THE ART & SCIENCE OF INTERNET CAR SALES

Understanding How to Communicate and Sell Cars & Trucks in the New Electronic Marketplace

Everything You Always Wanted to Know About Internet Car Sales (But Didn't Know Where to Ask)

Contents

INTRODUCTION

As I sat down to write this new introduction I realized I have now been selling and/or consulting in the Internet car sales arena for more than 10 years. Wow, so much has changed. Viewed with today's eyes the tools and communication styles we used in the past range from quaint to cringe worthy. But one thing that has not changed is dealerships' overall inability to deliver a consistently professional shopping experience to Internet customers. This book is an attempt to help with that problem.

The magic formula for success in Internet car sales is not magic at all, of course. At its highest level it's just "Provide your customers with the shopping experience you would want if you were the customer." Why should that be so hard? Yet it is.

Most dealers get hung up on these three obstacles:
1. How do we do it? What are the steps for going about it?
2. How do we get salespeople to learn the Sales process and then stick with it?
3. How do we give info and pricing over the Internet and still make gross?

We are going to spend most of our time in this book addressing these questions. Whether you are brand new to the biz or are a veteran Internet/BDC salesperson I think you will find valuable instructional content here.

After 26 years of inside and outside sales (houses, multimedia services, software and cars) I became a salesmanship and communications skills best practices consultant in 2010. Every week I am in car dealerships watching, listening, teaching, training, and helping them improve their Internet departments and BDCs. So you can be assured that the information herein is up-to-date real world stuff that works.

I hope you enjoy what follows.

Section 1:

THE WHAT & THE WHY

s changed the retail car business,
we did not send emails, today we
:ernet has brought to our industry
ctronic communications mediums.

oday Without First Using the
Any and all products at every price
point are now viewed on a screen before they are seen in person at a
store. This means today's retail shopping experience includes an extra
step that did not exist before. This phenomenon, nicknamed *Zero
Moment Of Truth* or *ZMOT* in 2011, is explained well and in great detail
in Google's free e-book "Winning The Zero Moment Of Truth." If
you are not already familiar with the concept I highly recommend you
take a moment to look over one or all of these essential pages.
http://www.zeromomentoftruth.com
https://www.thinkwithgoogle.com/research-studies/2011-
winning-zmot-ebook.html
https://www.thinkwithgoogle.com/research-studies/zmot-auto-
study.html

2). Everything You Do Is Now Public Knowledge. Before a
shopper ever comes to your dealership he/she is online learning not
only about your products but also about your store, especially the
reviews from your satisfied and unsatisfied customers. Suddenly,
"word of mouth" has gone from being one-on-one to one-on-
thousands.

**3). You Are Now Evaluated On Your Ability As A
Communicator.** We've already established that most customers' first
encounter with your store (and, therefore, the moment of impact that
forms their all-important first impression of your business) now occurs
online, and not in your showroom or outside your building. So how
does your dealership come across on your website? In your outbound

emails? On consumer review sites? What does your online presence say about you and your store? What is your narrative? Do you own your brand? What is your brand? Are you in control of your message, or is the message unintentionally controlling you?

4). Prospect Management Is No Longer Optional. Every name and email address in your contact management system today represents either a sales opportunity or a marketing opportunity. Effectively managing and utilizing your prospect and customer contact data is imperative if you are to maximize your message impact and harvest the sales hiding inside your database.

WHAT IS INTERNET SALES?

We are going to use the phrase "Internet sales" a lot in this book. Most of us use it to mean responding to incoming eLeads (electronic form leads) and working them to a sale. But, by strict definition, that is not Internet sales.

When customers go to your website, purchase the car they want sight unseen and then either have it shipped to them or come by to pick it up – that's true Internet sales, AKA eCommerce. If you are like most of us, you spend very little, if any, of your time doing this. You actually spend the majority of your time selling sales appointments.

With some exceptions, the real sale occurs at the retailer's place of business. But every exchange between buyer and seller prior to that visit can be conducted via phone, fax, email and text if the customer prefers. The salesperson's goal is getting the customer to come to the store for a face to face encounter.

So what most of us do is not really true Internet sales. It's electronic sales communications with purpose. And the purpose is securing a prospect appointment to visit the dealership. That is the type of Internet sales we are going to talk about here.

WHAT MAKES A GOOD INTERNET SALESPERSON?

Being a retail Internet automobile salesperson requires a certain amount of skill in:

- Written Communications
- Telephone Communications
- Prospect Data Management
- Salesmanship

It is not necessary to be extremely talented or experienced in all four areas to work in Internet car sales. If management at your store or auto group has a good grasp of creating successful Internet sales communications, has put together an effective *1st Response and Long Term Follow-Up Process* in a CRM, and knows how to motivate its team to continually follow the process, then all you have to do is make the calls and send the emails as prompted, use the templates provided, and follow the process. You will be guaranteed a certain level of success.

The prospect management component does require that Internet salespeople be disciplined and able to perform repetitive tasks each day. For this reason classic ADHD-type showroom sales stars often make poor Internet salespeople.

The showroom/floor salesperson begins each day asking, "What can I do to sell a car today?" The Internet car salesperson (especially the new car salesperson) instead asks "What can I do today that will help me sell a car today and another one the day after that? And the day after that? And the day after that?" Whereas showroom/floor selling is pretty much all tactical, Internet sales is both tactical and strategic. Therefore, the ideal Internet salesperson is a combination left-brained/right-brained person, a disciplined strategist who at the same time is creative and has people skills. This ideal candidate is often hard to find. (As a general rule women seem to be better at this than men, perhaps explaining why you see more women in Internet/BDC departments than on the sales floor.)

Some people mistakenly assume that Internet car sales is easy, that you just sit in your chair all day and stare at a screen while sales opportunities wash over you. But in fact, Internet sales is often harder than floor sales because the Internet/BDC salesperson does not have the advantage of face to face contact with the customer and does not have the physical product at hand. The Internet/BDC person has to build trust and an emotional connection with the customer (tangible intangibles) solely through the use of written word and voice. And so, never underestimate the importance of good salesmanship skills in Internet car sales. It is as necessary here as it is in any other form of selling.

WHAT WORKS BEST: BDC? DEDICATED INTERNET DEPARTMENT? SOMETHING ELSE?

Nobody has yet come up with the perfect set-up for Internet sales staffing. There are many approaches and all have their strengths and weaknesses.

Here are five approaches we've seen in daily use, with the first two by far the most common:

1). DEDICATED INTERNET SALESPEOPLE: Work the prospects from lead arrival to delivery.
- Upside: Salesperson is empowered to provide any and all information the customer wants/needs in order to get to the sale. Customer develops a trust relationship with the salesperson that continues all the way to delivery.
- Downside: Salesperson is often busy with test drives and deliveries when eLeads come in; fresh leads sit unanswered for long periods of time and long term sales follow-up also suffers.

2). BDC (acronym for Business Development Center):
Communications center, works each lead to appointment stage only.

- Upside: since personnel spend all day in front of their computers and phones eLeads are guaranteed a fast response and multiple contacts.
- Downsides: BDC personnel often must rely on floor salespeople or sales management to locate vehicles, price vehicles, and/or inspect and report back to the BDC before prospects can get the information they requested. Miscommunication and/or slow follow-up replies to customers can result. Prospects are handed off to a salesperson once they show up at the store; potential for miscommunication or customer mistrust and discomfort.

The BDC model works best when the staffers are knowledgeable about the products and the elements of the sale. Internet car buyers do <u>not</u> want to interact with someone who is essentially a receptionist or appointment taker.

3). INTERNET DESK TIME: Showroom salespeople receive Internet leads during appointed daily or weekly "Internet desk time" shifts. They return to showroom at end of shift but get to keep and work all leads received during desk time.

- Upside: eLeads are guaranteed a fast and quality first response from a salesperson empowered to provide any and all info customer wants/needs in order to get to the sale.
- Downside: Additional contact attempts/follow-up not guaranteed because salespeople are also working the floor, taking test drives and making deliveries.

4). INTERNET TEAM: Duo or trio with each member responsible for specific components of the sales process. (i.e. one team member handles all 1st Response & Follow-Up, the other team member handles all test drives, closes and deliveries).

- Upside: eLeads guaranteed fast and quality first response and follow-up, plus they get a salesperson empowered to provide any and all info customer wants/needs in order to get to the sale.

- Downside: Team members are "married" and must get along. All sales credits and commissions shared: concept runs contrary to car sales' culture of individualism.

5). ALL-INTERNET STORE: All showroom salespeople trained on handling Internet leads – there is no "Internet Department." Central point person(s) receives every eLead, qualifies it, and then immediately distributes it to an available trained floor salesperson for 1st Response & Follow-Up.

- Upside: eLeads are guaranteed fast and quality first response from a salesperson empowered to provide any and all info customer wants/needs in order to get to the sale.
- Downside: Additional contact attempts/follow-up not guaranteed because salespeople are also working the floor, taking test drives and making deliveries.
- Additional downside: monitoring and managing the activities of a large team of combo floor and Internet salespeople can be labor intensive. (Think herding cats.)

WHAT DOES THE INTERNET / BDC DEPARTMENT MANAGER DO?

There are as many possible Internet Director and/or Internet Sales Manager or BDC Manager configurations as there are Internet department structures. Some are selling managers, others are desking managers, others are I.T. systems administrators, some are marketing managers, and others are trainers and coaches. These are but a few examples we have seen.

Regardless of the store's Internet department set up, one thing we know for certain is that somebody, be it the department manager, the manager's assistant, or some other designated person (or combination of people) in the store must be tasked with the following:

- Combing through the CRM throughout the day to be sure salespeople's scheduled follow-up activities are completed. Although a salesperson might be out on a customer test drive, delivering a car, taking his/her day off, or whatever prospect follow-up must continue on schedule. When the assigned salesperson is unavailable someone else needs to maintain the sales momentum and complete the follow-up tasks due.
- Ensuring that incoming phone calls and Live Chat requests don't go unanswered during business hours and that voice messages do not languish unreturned.
- Ensuring that the store's call-to-action ($) bulk (blast) emails are composed and sent according to schedule.

The Internet car sales job, by its very nature, can be very rote and repetitive. As a result, opportunities to circumvent boredom will eventually prove too strong for most salespeople to resist. They will begin to second-guess and/or sidestep the Internet sales process, cherry pick and/or pre-qualify leads, and otherwise stray from the proven successful path to the sale. Accept this as fact. Someone representing management must regularly monitor the staff's activities daily to be sure this fallout does not occur.

DO WE HAVE TO STAY THE COURSE?

Yes. Regardless of how your store decides to operate it is imperative that you have an Internet strategy of some kind and that, once it is launched, you hold true to it. Making small adjustments and corrections from time to time is expected, but you must leave your overall plan in place for a minimum of 90 days while your strategy matures. *Do not change course during the 90 day start-up period!* This is very difficult for many dealers as it runs counter to their ever-changing / always-reactive store culture and nature. However, we can tell you with certainty that it is mandatory if you want the department launch/re-launch to succeed. Stick to your plan for a minimum of 90 days and, if necessary, up to 180 days. Stay the course.

HOW MANY LEADS CAN ONE PERSON WORK?

Rule of thumb: if your dedicated Internet department salespeople work the sales from beginning to end they should be able to competently manage 80 – 100 new leads (new car, used car, or combination) each month. If they work leads to appointment stage only (BDC) they should be able to handle 180 – 200 new leads each month.

HOW DO INTERNET PROSPECTS DIFFER FROM WALK-IN PROSPECTS?

While we can't claim that all Internet and walk-in shoppers differ in the ways we are about to describe, the comparisons below will help you understand how Internet and walk-in customers can have differing sets of expectations.

In the classic showroom sales set-up, the customer walks in the door to the dealership and is greeted by a salesperson. The talk quickly turns to the customer's vehicle of interest which (hopefully) leads to the test drive phase of the sales encounter. Hoping to "land him/her on a car" the salesperson takes the prospect on a test drive, the customer (hopefully) receives a professional quality drive and walk-around, and the two return happy to the dealership. The salesperson then turns to the customer and says, "Shall we make this one yours today?" At which point the customer says, "Well, not so fast...." Now the salesperson's work begins; we've entered the obstacles and objections phase.

In many cases, however, the Internet customer turns this formula around: *he/she wants to get the obstacles and objections phase out of the way first.* This explains why prospects like to self-educate themselves on their current vehicle's trade-in value, why they ask for monthly payments information in an email, and why they say they "don't want to waste time coming in to your dealership" until they receive a $ quote and all the cumbersome and unpleasant elements of the vehicle purchase are satisfactorily resolved first.

The salesperson (and/or BDC person's) goal is to get the appointment, and the way to get the appointment is to ease the anxieties that are keeping the customer from coming in to the store. So whereas your goal is to get the appointment, your job is to solve the Internet customer's problems, thereby easing his/her anxieties. Do that and the appointment part will take care of itself.

WHERE DO eLEADS COME FROM?

Every Internet sale starts with a sales lead. There are new car sales leads and there are used car sales leads. But where do they come from? Not every prospect finds you via your dealership's website or your listing on Autotrader. How many different lead sources and lead types are there? A lot.

The most common lead sources are
- Manufacturers (OEM) Websites
- Dealership Websites
- 3rd Party eLead Aggregators
- Affinity Programs
- Buyer Shopping Services
- Membership Programs
- Finance Applications
- Autotrader / cars.com / similar sites
- eBay / CraigsList / similar public sale sites
- Trade-In Valuation Sites

Prospects send you their eLeads from various sources, each prospect coming to you with his/her own agenda, and each lead source site having its own way of setting the customer's expectations. Therefore, all leads are not the same. Some people came to you because they pushed a button saying "Get Your Internet Price Quote." Others clicked "Get More Information." Still others pressed "Make An Offer" or maybe "Search Local Dealer Inventories" or "Name Your Price" or even "Get Three Dealers To Fight For Your Business" or who knows what. And there are many more. It is important to understand where a lead comes from and what expectations the customer has based upon when and where he/she submitted the eLead.

Manufacturers (OEM) Website
(OEM is an acronym for "Original Equipment Manufacturer)
Every manufacturer has a national public website presenting and promoting its products, and every new car dealer benefits by being tied to its manufacturer's public site. Interested prospects can find your store here after doing vehicle research and educating themselves on the products. Every manufacturer's site is unique, and if you have not yet gone to your manufacturer's site to experience it do so right away. Act the role of an interested shopper, see what you can learn about your brand vehicles, and then note the multiple opportunities the site offers you to contact a local dealership. Send yourself some test leads: what expectations did the pages set for you before you clicked the "Submit" button? Were these customer expectations then conveyed to you when the lead arrived in your CRM?

Dealership's Website(s)
This is your store's very own website or websites. Within this category there are actually two subcategories: OEM dealership sites and 3rd party dealership sites.

- **OEM dealership sites** are sites provided to new car dealers by the manufacturer. All manufacturers provide a "one size fits all" site to their agency dealers. Since all dealers in the manufacturer's national network get a version of the same site, these sites can be somewhat homogenous or generic looking, although most manufacturers allow the dealerships some level of customization and personalization of their site. Many smaller market stores use the manufacturer provided website as their only site. Act the role of an interested shopper, roam the site, see what you can learn about your inventory, and then note the multiple opportunities the site offers you to contact your dealership. Send yourself some test leads: what expectations did the pages set for you before you clicked the "Submit" button? Were these customer expectations then conveyed to you when the lead arrived in your CRM?

- **3rd party dealership sites** are sites created by an outside vendor at the request of a dealership. If your store has its own unique website, i.e. one not connected to the manufacturer, it's because your dealership contracted with a website developer to build and launch (and possibly maintain) the site. Some 3rd party dealership sites are completely unique and one-of-a-kind, but most come from established 3rd party website development vendors. If you have not explored your dealership's site(s) do so right away. Again, act the role of an interested shopper, see what you can learn about your store's inventory, and then note the multiple opportunities the site offers you to contact the store. Send yourself some test leads: what expectations did the pages set for you before you clicked the "Submit" button? Were these customer expectations then conveyed to you when the lead arrived in your CRM?

3rd Party eLead Aggregators. These can also be described as purchased leads and are not to be confused with 3rd party dealership website leads. 3rd Party eLead aggregators are "middle men" companies that collect interested prospects' names and contact info and then sell them to manufacturers and dealerships. There are many, many sources for these leads; most come from websites promising consumers research and/or comparison shopping answers. These companies are not directly affiliated with the manufacturers whose information they present, and many of these sites exist mainly to collect prospects' name and contact info and then in turn sell it to dealers. If you have not explored the many 3rd party car websites out there do it now. Act the role of an interested shopper and, starting with a Google search for your vehicle of interest, see what you can learn about today's Internet car research and shopping experience. Once you stray from the OEM and dealership websites you will find a jungle of sites promising (but sometimes not delivering) a wide array of pricing and other valuable information to info-hungry car shoppers.

Affinity Programs

These are most commonly employer-related discount programs. For example; some large corporations offer their employees pre-arranged discounted new car retail pricing programs for various products, retailers and/or manufacturers. Also, US military members have an affinity program through USAA.

Buyer Shopping Services

These companies offer new car buyers the ability to acquire a guaranteed competitive no-negotiations-needed price on a vehicle before the buyer visits a dealership. Some, like Edmunds.com and Consumer Reports, are primarily vehicle research and comparison sites. Others, like True Car, are primarily shopping services. Note that True Car also manages other companies' affinity programs, including those of USAA, Allstate, Geico, American Express and Consumer Reports.

Membership Programs

These are very similar to affinity programs though they are not related to specific employers or corporations. For example, pre-arranged discounted retail new car pricing is available for a small fee to anyone belonging to Sam's Club, Costco and some other discount clubs. In addition, many credit unions offer pre-arranged discounted retail new car pricing programs to their members. There are others.

Finance Applications

This is the prospect that completes a credit application before anything else. Sometimes these leads arrive with no vehicle of interest listed. Often this is a customer who first wants to know (or needs to know) if he/she is financeable before proceeding to select a car or truck.

Autotrader / cars.com / similar sites

Dealerships pay a fee (per vehicle listed or by subscription) to feature their vehicles on these popular public marketplace sites. These are predominantly used car and truck leads (some dealerships feature their new vehicles here also).

eBay / CraigsList / similar sites

eBay is the popular and well-established national public auctions site. CraigsList is an online free classifieds advertising site with local editions in most larger cities.

Trade-In Valuation Sites

These sites allow consumers to get sight-unseen data-driven automated trade-in value estimates for their current cars and trucks. When the consumer enters his/her info and clicks the "get my trade-in value now" button a lead is generated and sent to your store. Note that the lead may or may not include info on the new vehicle the consumer wants to buy - if, indeed, he/she does want to buy something. Black Book, KBB, NADA and Autotrader T.I.M. (Trade-In Marketplace) are some of the most popular sites.

HOW MANY TYPES OF eLEADS ARE THERE?

Regardless of the source, with few exceptions all of your incoming eLeads fall into one of only five categories:

1). New Car/Truck - General Inquiry
Provides name, contact info, plus (in most cases) year, make and model of vehicle desired - and little else.
2). New Car/Truck – In-Stock Unit Inquiry
Provides name, contact info, plus VIN or Stock # of the car or truck desired.
3). Used Car/Truck – In-Stock Unit Inquiry
Provides name, contact info, plus VIN or Stock # of the car or truck desired.
4). Credit App First.
The prospect begins everything by submitting a credit app.
5). Trade-In Valuation
Provides semi-detailed info on prospect's current car/truck - may or may not tell you what the consumer wants to buy to replace it.

Each lead type requires its own unique first response. Failure to send the correct response can result in a disgusted prospect. Always take care to read the lead and then send an appropriate first response. (More on this later).

ARE NEW CARS & USED CARS TREATED THE SAME?

No - selling new cars via the Internet requires a different approach from that employed to sell pre-owned cars. Used cars are often an easier and faster sell than new cars for reasons described below. They usually contain greater profit too.

USED: A used car is a one-of-a-kind item – no two used cars, even if they are the same year/make/model are identical. Therefore scarcity creates urgency as the customer realizes that he/she might have to purchase this vehicle right now or someone else will.

- VERSUS –

NEW: A new car is a considered a commodity – the prospect thinks there's no scarcity, and that the dealer can always locate another one or the factory can always build another one if necessary. The new car buyer might spend months researching the products and making the purchase decision.

USED: It's a level playing field - cars.com, autotrader.com, eBay.com (and others) have established and promoted their national online used car marketplaces where any dealer can offer his wares. The small rural store can put its inventory in front of just as many people as the big city store and at the same price.

- VERSUS –

NEW: There is no community marketplace – each dealer has to market and merchandise its own products and store via its own websites, banner ads, paid search campaigns, etc. Size of inventory and size of marketing budget can give big stores an advantage when selling new vehicles online.

DO INTERNET NEW CAR CUSTOMERS SHOTGUN THEIR INFO TO MULTIPLE DEALERSHIPS?

In a word, no. A few will do it, yes, but not a majority. The belief that all Internet customers submit their info to multiple dealers is a carryover from a decade ago when the Internet was still very new and dealers had not yet figured out how to react to it.

For example, in years past it was thought that fewer than 40% of the people who submitted eLeads to dealerships received an email reply of any kind. Prospects discovered that they had to submit to multiple dealerships if they wanted to get a response from even one.

At the same time, dealerships were awakened to the fact that, thanks to the Internet, interested customers now had access to wholesale vehicle information never before made so widely public. Some dealers reacted defensively, convinced that all Internet buyers were grinders committed to pitting dealers against each other in a race to the cheapest price.

Current data suggests that 10% - 20% of interested new car prospects will submit a request for price or information to more than one store at a time. In our experience that 10% - 20% is mainly made up of:
- Serious buyers ready to launch sales negotiations, and
- Information seeking prospects who do not receive the info they requested from Dealer A and so try again with Dealer B.

Think about your own online shopping behavior: do you like to spend hours and hours going from one retailer's website to another? Or are you satisfied once you find one that provides you the products and information you are looking for? Internet shoppers want quick clear results; when they submit to your store they are giving you the opportunity to delight them right away. If you do, they are happy and many will stay with you. However, if you disappoint them, they move on immediately and you have little chance of recapturing them.

WHAT IS AN INTERNET LEAD (eLEAD)?

IS AN eLEAD AN "UP"?

Yes. Treat it like one. In most cases an eLead is one of two things:

1) A person contacting you because they are ready to engage in sales negotiations, or,
2) A person contacting you because they want information to help them complete their research.

WHAT DO THEY WANT?

Most of the time you won't know. Not at first. When consumers use the Internet to research a big ticket purchase they are seeking answers to five essential questions, usually in this order.

1. What's the best made product(s) of this type in this class?
2. What size/shape/configuration of this product will work best for me?
3. Can I afford it?
4. Where should I buy it?
5. Am I getting a good deal?

The highest "high funnel" customers are working on the answer to question 1. Once satisfied with the answer to 1 they seek an answer to number 2. Once satisfied with the answer to 2 they seek an answer to number 3, bringing them to the mid-funnel stage. They become low funnel shoppers (i.e. highly likely to buy and buy soon) when they seek the answers to questions 4 and 5, thereby completing all 5 steps.

When the Internet lead arrives it is difficult, if not impossible, for you to know anything more about the customer than their name and contact info plus the year/make/model vehicle of interest. Therefore, your first job as the Internet salesperson or BDC salesperson is to

- Make contact with them, and
- Ask questions whose answers will enable you to understand
  - Which stage (1-5) the customer is in at the moment?
  - What objectives and desires are driving their pursuit of this vehicle purchase? (What are they trying to accomplish?)

Only then can you know how to sell them.

HOW DO WE CONTACT THEM?

You reply using all available media until you connect with the prospect.

- Email
- Phone
- Text Message

In the second half of this book we provide detailed examples of first response emails plus phone and text messaging scripts that you can use to make the all-important first contact with new prospects.

WHAT ARE THEY TELLING US?

When prospects send their personal contact info to a store or other business they are (usually) stating their case and asking for a response. Depending upon where they are in the buying funnel (low, mid or high) they are sending you one of two messages:

- I AM A GATHERER: I am still in the collecting information stage. I might not want to talk on the phone and/or have a direct relationship with you – not yet, anyways. But by giving you my contact info I am telling you that I want to stand downstream of your present and future communications flow as long as it is relevant to me. Please reply with the info I requested. *(High to mid funnel.)*
- I AM A SORTER: I am finished gathering info and doing research; I am now working my short list. I am ready to make a purchase or very close to it. Here is what you need to know about me now. Please read it over, utilize what I have given you, and respond via most appropriate method with the info I requested. *(Low funnel.)*

Sorters are likely to engage you in selling negotiations. Gatherers are not. Gatherers are often immune to hard selling offers - instead, they are seeking information/education, and a dealer with whom they can establish a trusting relationship.

When we receive the eLead we do not know which category it fits into, Sorter or Gatherer? Therefore we have to cover our bases and respond as though the sender is both prospect types at the same time. Instructions for doing this appear in the second half of the book.

WHAT PERCENTAGE WILL RESPOND?

The answer to this varies wildly, and few stores track this statistic. (They should.) Most dealerships we speak to feel that something between 15% - 40% of incoming eLeads become responsive prospects. Good news: as a professional sales communicator you have a lot of control over this number. (More on this to follow).

WHAT PERCENTAGE WILL BUY?

Again, this number can vary wildly. Many factors come into play, including those outside the dealer's control, like local market conditions, inventory, competitive market situation and others. In our experience, new car leads can be expected to close, on average, somewhere between 7% - 15% (although some new vehicle leads can close much higher). Used car leads are generally stronger - a 13% - 20% closing rate is not uncommon. Plus, some lead sources are better than others. Leads from a dealer's website, for example, typically close much higher than 3rd party provided leads. The target closing ratios for your store are unique to your store and must be calculated on an individual dealership basis.

If the percentage of eLeads who respond to you is, say, 25% (a hypothetical number in this example) and the averaged new car + used car closing ratio is, say, 12.5% (also a hypothetical number), then 50% of the prospects who respond to you will become a buyer – either at your store or at a competitor's. Therefore, the more prospects you can get to respond to you, the more you will sell. Simple as that.

WHEN DO THEY BUY?

Some Internet shoppers buy right away, some take their time. Used car buyers typically act faster than new car buyers. In most of the new car/truck stores we visit we find that, of the Internet prospects who become buyers, 35% - 50% buy within 1 – 5 days after submitting a lead, with another 10% - 25% completing their purchase by Day 10. (Shopper behavior varies according to dealership, market area, and vehicle price level, brand and type. Analyze your store's unique data to learn when your buyers buy).

A typical days-to-the-sale breakdown might look like this:

- 43% sales (sold by dealer or lost to rival dealer) = Day 1 – 5
- 21% sales (sold by dealer or lost to rival dealer) = Day 6 – 10
- 11% sales (sold by dealer or lost to rival dealer) = Day 11 – 30
- 25% sales (sold by dealer or lost to rival dealer) = >Day 30
- Average day to buy for those >30 days: Day 70.

This is valuable data as it helps you understand how to make the best use of your selling and marketing time.

WHO ARE THEY?

An eLead is often not what it first appears to be. Let's say you work for a Ford dealer and you just got a lead on a new Ford Mustang. Is this a person who wants a new Mustang? Possibly, but it could also be:

- Someone who actually wants a used Mustang
- A 14 year old kid building his fantasy muscle car on your OEM's site
- Someone who already knows he/she is hopelessly upside down in their current vehicle and can't buy today but is wishing and hoping for a miracle rescue
- A parent or grandparent looking for a cheap used car for their teenager. (Why did they click on the new Mustang button? Who knows?)
- A future first-time car buyer trying to educate themselves on how car buying is done
- Someone who thought they were registering online to win a free iPad
- An English speaking child making inquiry for their non-English speaking parent
- A person whose lease isn't up for 2 years and is just window shopping
- A buyer (Yay)! But also a grinder. (Boo)
- A "Get me bought" with a <450 Beacon making their umpteenth desperate attempt to get a car loan from somebody, anybody
- Or one of at least 1,336,749 other possibilities that can be added to the list above.

Until you make direct connection with this prospect, you can't know who they are. Only a very small percentage will fill in the comments box and clearly lay out their case ("I want your best payment on this truck, I have a paid off 2006 Silverado to trade in, and I have a 650 credit score"). Most leads arrive with little clue for you as to

      1). Where they are in the shopping process and

      2). What they want to accomplish.

It is your job to find those two missing pieces of information!

WHY THE BIG HURRY?

In Internet time, a minute seems like an hour and a few seconds wait time is unbearable. (Think about it; how long do you allow the little hourglass or daisy wheel to spin before you give up in disgust and move on to a different page?).

Although the Internet prospect may not respond quickly to you (if at all) he/she nonetheless expects you to respond within a time frame that matches his/her attention span. This means that a slow response (1+ hour after lead arrival) runs the risk of being only slightly better than no response at all. All the studies conclude that he/she who responds quickly has the advantage in getting the prospect's attention. However, prospects quickly dismiss fast responses with no satisfying content. Therefore the *real* winner is the dealer who responds fast and who also provides information of value to the consumer.

WHY CAN'T MY PEOPLE JUST GET 'EM IN?

The above phrase is a favorite of sales managers who don't understand the logic of Internet shoppers.

Today's Internet car shoppers are self-educating themselves as much as they can, contacting retailers only when it becomes a necessary step toward reaching their purchase goal.

If you tell this customer you will not/cannot provide information of value until he/she comes to your store they will never come to your store.

The way the shopper sees it, if you (the dealer) are not helping him/her advance to the sale by providing information he/she needs then you are actually standing in the way of the sale.

Why would they want to do business with a store like that?

WHAT IS PROCESS & CONTENT?

Everything starts at the beginning and Internet car sales communication starts here.
- Process
- Content.

You've already seen the word Process used a few times in this book so it's a good idea to understand what both words mean in this context.

PROCESS: As used here the word Process means a logical, timeline-based prospect *1st Response & Long Term Follow-Up* schedule that cues the salesperson to which prospects need a follow-up call or email each day and what message needs to be delivered to each. The software tool that enables us to accomplish this is called a CRM (acronym for Customer Relationship Management) or contact management system. If set-up correctly, your CRM successfully mates a viable prospect *1st Response & Long Term Follow-up Process* with email (and sometimes phone) scripts (i.e. Content) you can employ when making follow-up attempts. Plus, the CRM maintains prospect activity histories, enables you to send bulk email blasts to the database, and allows you to run reports that we couldn't dream of before this technology arrived.

Even if you only get 2 new leads per day, and assuming that, say, only 8% of your eLeads are turning into sales, by the end of 4 weeks you have 36 active leads to manage. Within 90 days you have 140. That doesn't sound like a lot of leads to manage but it is; staying on top of even a small amount of leads for more than two or three days is nearly impossible without some type of contact management tool plus *1st Response & Long Term Follow-Up Process.*

Keep in mind that the CRM is not the Process; the CRM is the software system that manages your Process for you. Most dealers assume that, by signing up for a CRM (regardless of brand), they are also getting viable Internet (and other) sales processes included in the deal. Not so. The people and companies who build and install CRMs are good technology folks but for the most part they have never sold a car in their lives. It is up to you, the dealership, to see to it that good Internet Process and Content is built into your CRM.

The trick to Process is that it must be followed daily; a Process that is not enforced is no Process at all. There are no "days off" from Process. It is important to keep this in mind.

CONTENT: This is the information you are giving to your prospects via email and/or phone. Some or all of your email replies might be hand typed and personalized. Others, for the sake of timeliness and efficiency, might be "canned" (pre-written) email messages commonly called templates. If a prospect responds to your initial replies you may have no use for templates content at all. But if the prospect is non-responsive (and the majority are) templates will allow you to stay in front of him/her without having to hand type a personal email every single time.

This is worth noting: Process trumps Content. You can have a good Process and weak Content and still sell cars. But if you have good Content but no Process you will have mediocre results at best.

CAN WE ACTUALLY ADVANCE SALES MOMENTUM WITH EMAILS?

Yes! Emails are not just "word noise" that you throw at customers! We've all seen (and sometimes used) phone scripts. A good call script helps you maintain and advance the sales momentum. It does it by asking the targeted questions that get the answers that help you keep your prospect on the critical path to closing. You can employ the same logic with your email templates.

Consider that there are 3 key elements to most sales:
1). The vehicle the customer wants to buy,
2). The vehicle the customer wants to trade-in, and
3). The money the customer will acquire to pay for their purchase

Think back to your sales training when you were shown how all three of these elements above provide shoppers with both excitement <u>and</u> anxiety. For every happy thought the prospect has of driving his/her new car or truck he/she also has painful worries about the process of acquiring it.

- "Will they give me enough for my trade?"
- "Will I get a payment I can afford?"
- "Will I be able to get the exact car/truck I want?"
- "Will this car dealer hose me in the finance office?" Etc. etc.

Almost every prospect will be relieved (and therefore relaxed and appreciative) when a salesperson helps him/her ease the anxiety connected to these three elements. Effective email follow-up can lead prospects down the critical path to the sale by offering opportunities - opportunities to get answers and information to these critical components of the sale. In other words, <u>information that gives value.</u>

THREE EASY EXAMPLES:
1). "Do you have a trade-in? Want to know what it is worth today? A free, no obligation appraisal at our store takes only minutes."

2). "Would you like to know in advance what kind of financing you can get at Friendly Motors? Just click this link, fill-out the credit app and I'll get right back to you with answers"

3). "Are you too busy to come to our dealership for a test drive? Let me bring the car/truck to you."

Be creative and think of as many value providing messages as you can. Now save these, because they will soon form the basis of your catalogue of email follow-up templates.

Properly written follow-up emails always advance the sales momentum – they do it by giving the prospect value - value in the form of opportunity, i.e. information that enables the customer to advance him/herself to the next stage of the sale.

WHAT ARE THE SECRETS TO GOOD FOLLOW-UP?

No secrets, really, just principles. There are only two and they are very simple.

- Only make a follow-up phone call/send a follow-up email/send a follow-up text to either
  - Get information from the prospect, or
  - Give information to the prospect. And
- Never do both in the same phone call or email.

Think about it: if you have no info to give, and you have no info to get, then you have no business doing the follow-up because you have nothing of value to offer.

One communication = one message. And every communication must give value. Simple as that.

WHAT IS PERMISSION MARKETING?

The phrase "Permission Marketing" was popularized by Seth Godin's landmark 1999 book of the same name. "Permission Marketing" occurs when individuals willingly provide their contact info (at minimum an email address) to a seller or information provider, thereby giving that seller/provider permission to market to them electronically.

An eLead is a prospective customer who has reached out to you and given you permission to contact him/her in return. If the prospect is a Sorter he/she might be giving you permission to engage in sales negotiations – now. If the prospect is a Gatherer he/she might instead be only giving you permission to have a communication relationship. Note that this does not necessarily mean the prospect wants a two-way relationship. The Gatherer might instead be saying, "I just want to stand downstream of your information output. Please include me in your content flow."

The more you maintain the communication relationship with the Gatherers (and do it by giving value), the more you help them move themselves from Gatherer to Sorter, and the better your chances of becoming their seller when they are ready to buy.
Because email has the unique ability to mass message people and do it consistently, a careful seller can utilize email to establish and maintain a long term relationship with the Gatherer customer.

If you use email to consistently communicate with your collected CRM leads over a period of, say, 6 months, and your outbound communications always give value, you will discover that only a tiny portion of them (maybe 5%) will "opt out" and refuse your continued emails. The great majority of them, even though they are taking no sales action at the time, willingly continue to receive your electronic communications. In effect, they are giving you permission to have a continued electronic relationship with them. Utilize it!

IS THE MEDIUM REALLY THE MESSAGE?

For more than 100 years people have been witnessing news and entertainment on movie screens. For more than 50 years Americans have had televisions in their homes. In the last 15 years computer monitors have become ubiquitous. And now, with the affordability of high quality flat screen monitors, an explosion of electronic text and images has taken place. Today, you can't go into a bar, bus terminal, grocery store, airport, classroom, hotel lobby, doctor's office, restaurant, bedroom, barber shop, office or dealership lobby without encountering a flat screen monitor. They're everywhere!

The result of this 24/7 bombardment of electronic text and images is this: people today are exposed to so much high visual quality electronic media every day that they now expect professional looking content on their screens. Any screen. Every screen.

The homemade-looking email you just sent, the one with the vague or confusing message, syntax errors, broken links, amateurish images, misspellings, grammatical errors and font and spacing issues, no longer gets it.

Like it or not, once you put text and/or images onto a screen today you are in the professional electronic communications business.

MUST WE TAKE INTERNET SERIOUSLY?

You will never find a call center located in the middle of a retail sales floor; with all the in-store customer interruptions the call center people could not complete their incoming and outgoing phone tasks. The same is true of Internet; if your Internet/BDC people are dashing outside to wait on customers on the lot or assist customers on the floor, their first response and long term follow-up tasks will go unfinished and your Internet lead sales will suffer.

Understandably, in many small stores the Internet salesperson also works walk-in customers by necessity. But if your store receives enough eLeads each month to warrant a dedicated Internet salesperson or sales team or BDC then you need to have a dedicated Internet salesperson or sales team, a BDC or a properly managed All-Internet store

Section 2:
THE HOW TO

HOW TO RESPOND TO eLEADS

Let's start with five simple rules to live by:
1) *Respond quickly*
2) *Respond often*
3) *Always give value*
4) *Always be upbeat*
5) *Always advance the sales momentum*

These 5 Golden Rules will carry you a long way. Cut them out, paste them over your monitor and make them your daily habits.
1) <u>Respond quickly</u> – FQR (first quality response) email in < 1 hour every time
2) <u>Respond often</u> – Email + phone + text – touch the prospect often, until you find the medium that they prefer, so that they feel they are being courted
3) <u>Always give value</u> – In all your communications provide the prospect with opportunities to acquire knowledge and information that will lead him/her to the inevitable sale.
4) <u>Always be upbeat</u> – Never sound needy ("Am I emailing too much?") or irritated ("Is there a reason you have not called us back?") In all your communications convey the cheery, optimistic and unquestionable assumption that the prospect will be a customer – if not today, someday.
5) <u>Always advance the sales momentum</u> - Never throw a problem or decision back at the prospect and make him/her deal with it. (Example: "No, the one you asked about does not have a sunroof. Here's a link to our website so you can find something else.") As the salesperson it is <u>your</u> job to address the obstacle, step over it, and keep things moving forward. ("The one you asked about does not have a sunroof, but it has everything else. It is a beautiful XLT with media center, adjustable pedals, and tinted windows. Please let me show it to you.")

THE ALL IMPORTANT FIRST RESPONSE

It's corny, but it's true: you only get one chance to make a good first impression. This applies to Internet sales just as it does in the showroom.

The sale can be made or lost in the first hour: how you initially respond to a new lead is far more important than all of your (nevertheless important) follow-up efforts. Don't blow it coming out of the gate!

So - a new eLead has just arrived. What do you do? Here it is, in order:
1) Read the lead
2) Send a First Quality Response (FQR) email
3) Make the first phone attempt
4) Send a text message

1). **Read the Lead**
Believe it or not, failure to read the lead is the most common dealer error we encounter when doing mystery shops. This is especially true of new vehicle leads.

Remember that, regardless of source, with few exceptions all of your incoming eLeads fall into one of only five categories:
1) New Car/Truck - General Inquiry
Provides name, contact info, plus (in most cases) year, make and model of vehicle desired - and little else.
2) New Car/Truck – In-Stock Unit Inquiry
Provides name, contact info, plus VIN or Stock # of the car or truck desired.
3) Used Car/Truck – In-Stock Unit Inquiry
Provides name, contact info, plus VIN or Stock # of the car or truck desired.
4) Credit App First.
The prospect begins everything by submitting a credit app.
5) Trade-In Valuation
Provides semi-detailed info on prospect's current car/truck - may or may not tell you what the consumer wants to buy to replace it.

There is no one-size-fits-all response to a new lead. Each requires a reply tailored to the particular type of inquiry being made. And before you can do that you have to know exactly which type of eLead you are working with.

To the customer there's nothing worse than requesting X from the dealership only to have the dealership respond with Y. Example: a prospect sends you a new car VIN-specific inquiry and your first email reply says "I need more information before I can help you. Do you have a particular make, model or color in mind? Please call me at...." He already told you the VIN or stock number of the specific car he desires. Therefore, your reply can be interpreted as a ploy to get him on the phone without providing any information upfront. Or it could be seen as proof that you did not take the time to read his eLead before responding. He has now branded you as an "old school" car salesman who just wants to get him into the store and hose him. Or a sloppy loser who doesn't pay attention to business. Either way, you just made a terrible first impression on this prospect. *Read the lead!*

2). Send the First Quality Response (FQR) Email

- Respond Quickly. Responding to a fresh lead via email in less than one hour greatly multiplies your chances of a reply. Internet shoppers want info NOW, not 5 hours from now. If an hour or two has passed and they haven't heard from you they move on. He who responds fastest with a quality (i.e. value-giving) reply wins.

- Personalize The Email. We can't stress this enough; your efforts will fall flat if the prospect feels that he has received a form letter 1st response. (Fresh prospects are looking for a relationship first, and a car second. Form letters do not create relationships). Find some way to add a brief personal line or two to the beginning of the email, even if the lines are unrelated to the car deal. Say something/anything to let the prospect know that a real person has taken the time to read his inquiry and is replying with a personal touch.

- Fill-In the Blanks. 1st Quality Response templates should have sections that must be completed before sending; be sure every line is filled-in correctly and that any non-applicable wording is removed before sending the email. This is your one shot at making a strong positive first impression: take the extra few minutes and tailor the template to the customer's request. A great FQR email can keep you in or out of the game!

3). Make the First Phone Attempt

Notice that we are sending the FQR email first, then calling? Many stores like to call first, believing that a phone call trumps an email every time. And it's true; for immediacy and rapport building it's hard to beat a phone call. However, favoring the telephone can also cause problems:

- Whereas you the dealer prefer telephoning, your prospect may not. There is a good chance that the person who chose to send you an eLead when he/she could have called instead really wants and expects an email reply from you first instead of a call.

- You may call within minutes of receiving the lead and leave a message, believing that you have fulfilled your duty to respond quickly. Your CRM may even count the quick phone reply as a fast lead response time (LRT). But if you don't send an FQR email within minutes of completing your call the prospect expecting a prompt and informative written word reply is extremely disappointed at what he/she believes to be your very slow email response time, no matter how many phone messages you leave.

- If you phone first you have very little to say in your voice message (do not most calls result in a voice message?) except, "Hi James, Tom at Friendly Motors here, ready to talk about that Jetta you asked for. Please call me back at 555-5555" Whereas if you send the FQR email first you now have a valuable message to leave on the prospect's voice recorder ("Hi James, Tom at Friendly Motors here, I received your request and replied already with the very information you want. Please check your email and please let me know if you do not have it.") Your voice message just gave value!

When an eLead arrives in your CRM you can't know if it is a phone-centric prospect or an email-centric prospect. Therefore, you have to give equal attention to both mediums right from the start. (Actually three mediums; if you aren't yet using text messaging start now).

If you send the email first you are giving the prospect what logic says he or she asked for, thereby completing your half of the implied agreement. You have now earned the right to pick up the phone – and also to ask for the appointment.

4). Send A Text Message

Are you still debating whether to employ text messaging in your eLead response process? The debate stops now. Just do it.

- Text messages get through when other communication mediums do not. Example: in 2016 we had numerous incidents where our mystery shopper thought he had been ignored by a dealer, only to receive a text from the salesman saying "I replied right away by email. Please let me know if you didn't get it." A quick check of the Spam folder (buried below the bottom of the screen in many email apps) showed that the dealer had indeed sent his FQR promptly, we just didn't know it. If he hadn't sent that text....

- Although we can't remember the source, we have heard it said that the average email gets a response within 48 hours. And the average text message gets a response within 4 minutes. Which response time do you prefer?

- One of our Oklahoma dealers tracks everything. He recently showed us a monthly report that said his salesmen's outbound emails got replies 25% of the time, whereas their outbound text messages got replies 50%+ of the time. Which response rate do you like best?

- Sending vehicle photos and/or a short video via text is a fantastic way to make a connection with the prospect. It tells the customer that you care about providing a pleasant and informative shopping experience.

Today, few leads come with a landline phone number. When you have a cell number to both call <u>and</u> text why not utilize it?

Note about texting permissions: in 2011 Lithia Motors paid $2.5 million to settle a class action suit asserting that Lithia spammed 58,000 customers/prospects with unwanted text messages. Influenced by this event the Telephone Consumer Protection Act (TCPA) was amended in 2013 to address the issue of spam texting. The rules wording is considered ambiguous by many and there are conflicting interpretations as a result. Most CRM manufacturers interpreted the rule to mean that calls/texts sent from software products/devices (that would include CRMs then) must have written consent (i.e. opt-in) from the consumer before they can be sent, whereas calls/texts manually sent from individuals' phones do not. (The spammers and scammers who call and text me every day must have decided not to read the TCPA.) A quick Google search will provide much greater explanation than provided here. Do the small amount of research necessary to familiarize yourself with the TCPA then act as you see fit.

WHAT MAKES A GOOD FQR (First Quality Response) EMAIL?

In the majority of cases, prospects complete a lead form and submit it because their Internet research has brought them to a wall. In other words, they have self-educated themselves all they can on their own from websites and now need to communicate with a human being at a dealership in order to get to the desired next stage in their research.

When the Internet salesperson responds with a message that says only "Thank you for your request. Please call me so we can discuss" and/or ignores the direct question in the prospect's submittal the salesperson really hasn't given the prospect anything of value, i.e. he/she hasn't given the customer anything that the customer can't already discover through his/her own web research. So why are we disappointed when the customer does not respond?

In almost all cases a first quality response (FQR) email must contain the four (or more) core elements that give value to the customer. To illustrate this point, allow us to first tell a brief story.

THE SHOE STORE (A True Story)

We recently assisted an area dealership that experimented with launching a BDC. They staffed this communications center with four young women, all of whom had a small amount of prior work experience but no car business experience. The savviest of the four had been an assistant manager at a chain shoe store. When I stopped in after a few weeks to inquire on the BDC's progress she said to me, "This car business is weird. These old car dogs here wouldn't last a day at my former shoe store." I asked her to explain.

"Imagine a customer walks into a shoe store and says 'I'm interested in a pair of men's black dress shoes'. Pretty common, right? Happens every day. Here's how we were taught to respond to that customer:"

1) "Great! I am thrilled to be of help."
Acknowledge the customer and show enthusiasm

2) "We have a great selection of men's black dress shoes."
Confirm availability of the product so customer knows he/she is in the right place.

3) "In fact, we have (BRAND NAME SHOE) on sale this week for only $XX.XX."
Make an offer to sell something – let the customer know your store has sales

4) "Follow me this way and we'll try on some shoes."
Lead the prospect to the next step in the sale, the hands-on experience.

"But," she said, "If one of these old car dogs here had to work at a shoe store it would go like this:

CUSTOMER: "I'm interested in a pair of men's black dress shoes."
OLD CAR DOG SALESMAN: "Sure, I'll need a little more information before I can help you."

- Are you looking for leather sole shoes or rubber shoe shoes?
- Do you want slip-ons or lace shoes?
- Do you want round toes, square toes or wing tips?
- Are these formal dress shoes or casual dress shoes?
- Do you have a pair of shoes to trade-in?
- Are you already working with someone else at our store?
- And are you planning to pay for this with cash, check, a debit/credit card or are you interested in financing with us?

Her joke was painfully on target. How many times have we all acted exactly like the old car dog in the example above? We get an eLead that says only "2017 GMC Sierra" and we immediately send the customer an email that grills him with questions:

- Do you want the V6 or the V8?
- What trim line do you like best?
- What colors are important to you?
- Are you already working with somebody else at this dealership?
- Do you have a trade-in? Has it been appraised?
- Are you planning to finance? If so, do you have some idea of what your credit score is?

In our efforts to get right to the close we end up slapping the customer in the face with hard questions that he/she in all likelihood can't answer. And if the customer did know the answers to all these questions why would they need us? In our misguided effort to quickly land the customer on a car we waste the opportunity to provide value and service.

Remember, we are only valuable to the consumer when we provide solutions to the problems that caused him/her to reach out to us in the first place.

In the two shoe store scenarios described above which salesperson is more likely to make a sale today?

THE 5 ESSENTIAL ELEMENTS OF A GOOD FQR

In all but a few situations the perfect new car/truck FQR must have these five key components:

    1)   Brief, personalized and enthusiastic greeting

Acknowledge the customer and show enthusiasm

    2)   Confirmation of availability of product

"You are in luck! We have a great selection of _____ – or – We have access to a large selection of_____...." or something like that.

    3)   A photo or picture of the product.

Big is better – remember that the majority of recipients are reading this email on their smart phone. Teeny little postage stamp size pics/drawings do not get it.

    4)   An offer to sell something

"Here's a year/make/model we have on sale right now – or – We've got 0% for 72 months on this model through the end of the month only! – or – The manufacturer just added an extra $500 rebate on this model for the next 5 days!" or something like that.

    5)   Notification to the customer that you are going to maintain the sales momentum and advance him/her to the next stage of the sales process.

"I'll be calling you soon to be sure you got this email – or – I'll be calling you to set up a test drive" or something like that.

In the template example that follows you will see these concepts put into action. This is a **New Car/Truck General Inquiry FQR**: the lead gave only the prospect contact info and year/make/model new vehicle. That's it. How is that any different than "I'm interested in a pair of men's black dress shoes"? It's not. Here's a salesperson's sample first email response.

SUBJECT LINE: 2017 Chevy Cruze from Friendly Motors. (709) 709-7090

Hi James -

Good news! We have Chevy Cruze models in stock right now for you to see and drive.

Do you like this one? It is available and on sale:

2017 Chevrolet Cruze Hatchback
LS Automatic Stock #12345
Exterior color: Arctic Blue Metallic / Interior color: gray
Key options/upgrades/packages: power moonroof, navigation electronics package
MSRP +$00,000
Current factory-to-consumer discount/rebate incentives -$ 0,000
Friendly Motors special discount -$ 0,000
Your Friendly Motors sale price = $ 00,000 (+ TT&L).

Did you know? GMAC is offering 0% financing or $000 mo. lease special on this model too. This ends soon!

You can have a free, no obligation Chevy Cruze test drive today. Shall we make an appointment now? Or can I bring one by your home or workplace today instead?

I'll call you in a little bit to be sure you got this email.

Tommy Salesman

FQR RATER (First Quality Response Scoring Tool)

How good are your store's FQR emails? Do they pass the "Five Key Components" test? The FQR Rater form (below) enables you to score FQRs to insure that they give value to prospects. We use it when we evaluate mystery shops.

Try it: open your store's CRM and randomly read and score your salespeople's FQRs with this form. How many FQRs get a "Yes" on the majority of rows? The more "Yes" boxes you can check the better the FQR.

eLEAD DETAILS & FQR SCORE								
Prospect Name				Salesperson				
Lead Start Date		Lead Start Time				Date Contact Made		
Lead Type:	Dealer Sponsored Site: In-Stock VIN-specific			OEM site or 3rd party: No-VIN				
Button Shopper Clicked (Shopper Expectation):			Get ePrice	Request/Get Price/Quote			Buy It Now	
Dealer Price	Check Availability		Get/Request More Info		Schedule test drive			
Contact Our Team	Let Us Find It For You		Other					
Build Your Own: Get Internet Price		Build Your Own: Search Inventory			Build Your Own: Get Local Offers			
Vehicle of Interest	Year		Make		Model		Trim Line	
Color		Options/Packages						
*Question the shopper asked:								

FQR SCORING	Yes	No			
Was FQR sent within 1 hour?	Yes	No	LRT:	Hr	Min
Was the FQR personalized?	Yes	No	?		
Did the FQR show enthusiasm?	Yes	No	?		
Did the FQR acknowledge the shopper's question?*	Yes	No	?	N/A	
Did the FQR answer the shopper's question?*	Yes	No	?	N/A	
Did the FQR confirm availability of product?	Yes	No	?		
Did the FQR show & merchandise the product?	Yes	No	?		
Did the FQR make an offer to sell something?	Yes	No	?		
Did the FQR close with an advance to the next step of the sale?	Yes	No	?		
Did the FQR acknowledge the trade-in evaluation info provided?	Yes	No	?	N/A	

PUTTING PRICES IN EMAILS – THE PROS & THE CONS

To price or not to price? Few issues have been as hotly argued as this one.

Dealers who refuse to include pricing in an email usually say "Why should I provide a price if the customer did not ask for one?" Or they hold to the argument that if they do publish a price customers are just going to print that email, rush down to a competing dealership, and wave the page in front of another dealer's face and say "Can you beat this?" By refusing to send a price the dealership thinks it is protecting its opportunity to hold for gross on the prospect's possible sale.

Let's say that again; the store thinks it is protecting its opportunity to hold for gross on the prospect's possible sale.

You can already see that this logic is questionable. The dealer is passing up a likely sales opportunity (what you're trying to do is get the customer in the store, right?) in exchange for a possible sale that is likely im-possible because the dealer declined the sales opportunity!

In most cases the dealer who refuses to put a price in his emails is confusing giving a price with making an offer to sell.

Think about traditional newspaper, radio and television car dealer advertising; it screams "$10,000 Off MSRP!" or "Get This 2017 Ford F-150 STX only $ 23,999!" or "Lease for $299 Month with Only $1,000 Down!" or something similar. Does this type advertising give a price or does it make an offer to sell?

Internet customers are no more determined to get the lowest possible price than are showroom customers. While they don't want to discover that they paid too much, they don't mind paying a fair price. Yes, there are always going to be a small number of grinders who will drive clear across town to save $50 but this has been and will always be true. The majority of shoppers, showroom and Internet, will pay what in their mind is a fair price.

As we saw earlier, the Internet shopper wants to get the details stuff out of the way upfront, then come to the dealership. Therefore, if your FQR emails make no offer to sell, you are withholding a key component of the info the shopper wants and needs to see before he/she will come to your store. You just got crossed off the short list.

Here are just a few examples of scenarios where withholding a price in the FQR email can have negative results.

- Few buyers drive out of your store in the vehicle they came in to see. Many dealers argue, therefore, that it really doesn't matter what $ you put in your FQR email, no matter how heinous that $ might be to the dealership, because the customer ends up picking out another vehicle once he/she gets to your store anyway and when that happens negotiations start anew. (Plus you might get a trade-in you can hold on, plus you might get their financing business). But it was that price you included in the FQR, in concert with other elements that succeeded in getting the customer to come to the store. And isn't that really the goal of Internet sales?

- Refer back to the Shoe Store Story that appeared earlier in this book. How better to build sales excitement from the start than to tell the new customer that you have products on sale now? (Everybody loves a sale). And how far along the path to the sale can you get before price comes up anyway? So instead of avoiding the inevitable, present it proudly and be the first to do so. Your time-to-sale will decrease.

- The customer sends a lead to your store and another. Your FQR makes no mention of price save for MSRP, the other dealer shows MSRP and discounts. Which FQR is the customer more likely to reply to?

- Sometimes the customer is an immediate buyer, has already located the dealers who have the exact vehicle he wants, and is staging a price bake-off among multiple dealers. If you send him a written (email) price quote he will take your page and use it for price comparison with your competitors, true. But that's been his objective all along and in most cases he's made it clear from the start. He is not interested in your superior customer service, not interested in your free service shuttle, not interested in your free coffee, not interested in anything but who has "the best deal." If you refuse to send a price to this customer and instead try to cajole him into "coming on down" to your dealership for a visit you will be instantly eliminated from the contest and receive 100% of $000.00. You can opt out. If you are not interested in the grinder's business that's fine; simply let him know that. Reply and say "Thank you for your offer but we decline to participate."

Additional notes about giving a price in emails:

- When they clearly request a price you have no choice but to comply. If you withhold the info the prospect wants unless he agrees to come in, he won't come in. Period.
- The strong majority of new car leads are non-VIN specific, therefore, you can safely start off showing them an example of that model that you have on sale, then offer specifics.
- When a prospect asks your price on a specific new car VIN he is often just trying to understand how your store prices cars. (Most people do not end up buying the car they 1st requested a quote on anyway). Only a small percentage of buyers are true price grinders.
- Price is usually a compelling factor for the used car buyer. He/she expects the seller to lead off the price negotiations early in the game.

HOW TO WORK THE RESPONSIVE PROSPECT

Congratulations; the prospect you replied to yesterday wrote/called/texted you back in the wee hours or when you were otherwise unavailable. Now what do you do? Do you call? Do you write back? Ultimately, you have to use your own good judgment.

If the prospect responds to you by email...

This is good, though a bit tricky – it could be that he likes what you sent, but does not yet want to get one-on-one with you via telephone. Or it may just be easier for him to do the car deal after hours via email. Or maybe he is at work and needs to use a medium that does not involve making noise. You probably want/need to reply by email, at least for now. Note: be careful, because email always carries the potential for miscommunication due to poor word choice or misconstrued tone. Give the customer whatever he/she wants (within reason, of course) but measure your words carefully. Pause, re-read, and be certain your reply says exactly what you need/want it to say before you hit the "Send" button.

Note: Avoid the back-and-forth, back-and-forth email trap. You can email yourself right out of a relationship. Rule of thumb: if the customer writes and you reply, then they reply and you reply again, and then they reply again that marks 3 times the customer has replied via email. At this point stop emailing if at all possible and engage them on the phone. Too many email back-and- forths can become tedious and cause the prospect to lose interest (even though they started it). Also, the more you email back-and-forth the more risk that someone's tone or choice of wording will eventually be misunderstood, causing the relationship to sour.

If the prospect responds to you by telephone...

This could go well – the prospect likes what you sent and wants to get one-on-one with you on the phone. Work it according to what common sense and your good salesmanship skills tell you to do.

If the prospect responds to you by text....

This is very good; although the prospect is still using the written word to communicate with you versus real time verbal communication. Text messaging has an urgency and intimacy about it that makes it a powerful communication medium. The fact that he is using text to talk to you can be interpreted to mean that he is allowing you inside his private communication device; his smart phone. Keep every text communication brief and to the point. *Rule of thumb: text messages should be short enough that they can be read at a stop light.*

NOTE: two texting errors our mystery shoppers repeatedly see:

- If the shopper replies to the salesperson's text the salesperson immediately assumes that the customer only likes to text. From that point on the shopper gets too many texts, texts that are too long and complicated, or both. Don't stop using email and phone when the prospect responds to your texts. Use text to notify the customer that you sent him information via email or voice message. If she/he wants to engage you in further discussion via text then let them, of course.
- Always identify yourself when you text a prospect. Just because you had some exchanges yesterday, don't assume that he/she is going to recognize your number today. Our mystery shoppers have to text "Who is this?" a lot because salespeople don't ID themselves.

If the prospect responds by just showing up at your store...
Other than the fact that these surprise drop-ins can crater your activity plan for that day, this is the very best result you can hope for. You now have a customer in your showroom. Go sell!

HOW TO WORK THE NON-RESPONSIVE PROSPECT

You replied to yesterday's new eLead and did everything right. It's the next morning and still no reply. Now what?

The hard fact is most of the people who send in leads will not respond, no matter how good your first response process. So what about that majority of prospects who do not respond to you, at least not right away? Do you ignore them? Do you harass them? Do you delete them?

The answer is:
- You sell to the folks who respond to you.
- You market to the folks who do not. And,

- You rely upon your CRM's First Response & Long Term Follow-Up Process to help you do both.

Just because a prospect has, until now, been unresponsive, it doesn't mean that they are not a buyer, today or in the future. You don't yet know.

Recent Internet car shopper behavior data says that, depending upon your brand, store and market area, anywhere from 50% - 60% of your Internet leads who convert to buyers will do so within 5 – 10 days of submitting their lead. (We will assume this is true for the sake of this section). Logic says that, to increase your chances of connecting with those who are ready to be a buyer soon, you want to make as many contact attempts as is reasonably possible during this critical first 5 – 10 day period.

However, some buyers won't come around until well after 5 days – and as many as 25% of the buyers won't buy until well after 30 days.

You can't devote the same amount of attention to these late-comers as you must to the hot fresh prospects – but you can't afford to ignore these folks, either. The practical solution is to write a <u>1st Response & Long Term Follow-Up Process</u> that tasks salespeople with devoting ample personal attention to prospects in their first 1 - 5 days while automating (as much as is possible) an email follow-up schedule that lets you market to these unsold/unresponsive prospects after that time.

THE 1st RESPONSE & LONG TERM FOLLOW-UP PROCESS

Most CRM tools come from the factory pre-loaded with a default eLead handling Process plus some email templates Content. The Process and Content included with most CRMs is generic, outmoded and outdated stuff that is provided only so you will have something to run when you first turn on the system. It is highly unlikely that you want to use it. We recommend that you build your own Process and Content and structure them to match the days-to-the-sale demonstrated buying habits of your store's customers.

The two most common types of First Response & Long Term Follow-Up processes are
1. Timeline Based
2. Rules Based

The **Timeline Based** process is the easiest to write and manage. It assigns first response and follow-up tasks according to a fixed schedule that launches the day the lead arrives (if possible) or the following day. With a Timeline Based process, if for some reason a day's tasks are not completed, the next day you simply move on and complete the tasks scheduled for the current day. What's past is past.

The **Rules Based** process is more sophisticated. It says "On Day X you do this. Once you complete this task the next task in the process will reveal itself." In this case, if for some reason a day's task is not completed, the next day you must complete (or at least address) the previous day's task(s) before you can complete today's tasks also.

Each process type has its upsides and downsides. We like Timeline Based CRM processes because they afford salespeople more control and flexibility. But of course, "With great power comes great responsibility," so....

ILLUSTRATED EXAMPLE: 180 DAY 1st RESPONSE & LONG TERM FOLLOW-UP PROCESS ⟶

SUGGESTED 180 DAY 1st RESPONSE & LONG TERM FOLLOW-UP PROCESS

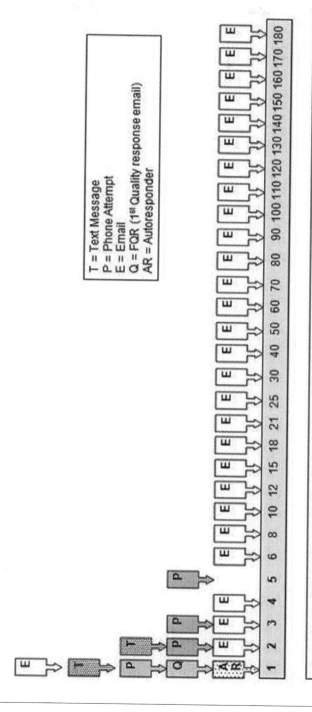

T = Text Message
P = Phone Attempt
E = Email
Q = FQR (1st Quality response email)
AR = Autoresponder

THE PROCESS SHOWN ABOVE SHOULD BE ACCOMPANIED BY A CONSISTENT TARGETED BULK EMAIL CAMPAIGN. (Minimum 1 X each month.)

There are many other 1st Response & Long Term Follow-Up processes out there – we happen to be fond of this one for a number of reasons. This all-purpose easy to use Timeline-Based 180 Day example works with both new and used car buyers. The point is to sell to prospects during the first (in this example) five days and if they remain unresponsive after that time then market to them thereafter.

Example: 1st Response & Long Term Follow-Up Process
Note that for the sake of simplicity and familiarity we are calling Day 1 the day of lead arrival. (Most CRMs call this Day 0.)

Day 1: The first item to go out is the Autoresponder, a 24 Hour Auto-Response Email – this is the prospect's "receipt" acknowledging that the dealer received the eLead. Autoresponders are optional; some stores like them as an after-hours acknowledgement, some like them 24/7, some don't like them at all. Your choice.

Next up:
- FQR (First Quality Response) template-based outgoing email. (Manual Send)
- 1st call attempt
- Text message
- "Did You Get My Reply?" – sent at end of the day if prospect has been unresponsive.

STEPS SHOWN BELOW APPLY TO ALL PROSPECTS WHO REMAIN ACTIVE YET UNRESPONSIVE.
If a prospect replies/responds immediately change his/her status to "Working" "Responding" "Contacted" "Appointment Set" or whatever CRM status applies.

Depending upon the prospect and their particular situation you may or may not wish to cancel the remaining Process steps shown below. But if the prospect remains unresponsive then definitely continue the schedule shown below until either direct contact is made or until you elect to drop manual follow-up and allow automation to take over. (In this example all manual follow-up ends after Day 5. Some dealers, depending upon staff quantity and quality like the automation to start earlier or later than 5 days.)

The suggested process steps shown here assume that the dealership has a portfolio of email templates that can be used for both manually sent emails and automatically sent emails. After the FQRs a dealership can get away with having only 8-10 additional templates as they can be repeated/re-used to fill out/complete the long term follow-up process.

- Day 2 – 2nd Quality Response Email
- Day 2 – Call attempt
- Day 2 – Text message (OPTIONAL)
- Day 3 – 3rd Quality Response Email
- Day 3 – Call attempt
- Day 4 – 4th Quality Response Email
- Day 5 – Call attempt

All remaining outgoing contact attempts are automated emails. Once template supply is exhausted (every template has been used once) it's OK to start at the beginning and repeat the templates sequence as many times as necessary in order to complete the schedule below. (Prospects will not notice that they are receiving the same template they received a few days/weeks ago.)

- Day 6 - Email
- Day 8 - Email
- Day 10 – Email
- Day 12 – Email
- Day 15 – Email
- Day 18 – Email
- Day 21 – Email
- Day 25 – Email
- Day 30 – Email
- Day 40 – Email
- Day 50 – Email
- Day 60 – Email
- Day 70 – Email
- Day 80 – Email
- Day 90 – Email
- Day 100 – Email

- Day 110 – Email
- Day 120 – Email
- Day 130 – Email
- Day 140 – Email
- Day 150 – Email
- Day 160 – Email
- Day 170 – Email
- Day 180 – Email

Bulk/Blast Emails - 5th day of each month send targeted email – and/or - 20th day of each month send targeted email

---

EMAIL TEMPLATES

Now that you have a process you know when to touch your prospects. So what do you say to them? This is where email templates come in handy.

Before we get into some template examples, know that there are no rules for creating good content, only principles. Good email content is composed of equal parts communication and salesmanship skills, mixed with an eye for basic (can be very basic) graphic design, and assembled with an awareness that "the media is the message." And, of course, your messages must be relevant to the recipient by giving value.

COMMUNICATION – The tone of the email goes a long way toward pushing the message across. For example, technology (email, chat, text) has caused our communications today to be increasingly informal, personal and brief. Whereas ten years ago formal-sounding business letters were the accepted response to customer inquiries, today short, informal email or text messages rule the day. Rule Of Thumb: if it looks good on a smart phone, it will look good everywhere. Make your templates clean, clear and concise – shorter is better than longer. And always test them on a smart phone before launching.

SALES MOMENTUM – Rule # 1! It is the salesperson's job to direct and maintain the sales momentum. The only person allowed to stop the sales momentum is the customer. Therefore, properly written follow-up emails must advance the sales momentum – they do it by giving the prospect value in each email - value in the form of opportunity for the customer to educate and (therefore) advance him/herself closer to the inevitable sale. (More on this below.) Rule # 2: in all your communications convey the cheery, optimistic and unquestionable assumption that the prospect will be a customer – if not today, someday.

DESIGN – Use fonts and spacings that are easy on the eyes, plus a simple one piece graphic header that pushes your store's brand (optional). Sans-serif fonts (Arial, Calibri and Tahoma are popular examples) look best on electronic screens. Serif fonts (Times New Roman, Courier, Garamond and hundreds of others) look best on the printed page and should be avoided. Note: be sure that every outgoing email uses the same graphic header, same font type and same font size. Employing these simple, basic branding techniques is the easiest way to establish brand familiarity (for you and the dealership) while also notifying prospects that you and your store are professional.

GIVE VALUE – you are going to get tired of hearing us say this but it cannot be ignored: all outbound messages must be relevant to the consumer and the way to be relevant is to give value. Think about this: every time we sit down to our computers or look at our phones we expect to be entertained, informed or both. A session in which we are neither entertained nor informed results in frustration. Let's use YouTube as an example: you click on a video that looks interesting, it plays, you like it, and now you feel different than you did when you first clicked on the vid. Success! *You feel pleasantly better now than you did when you started.* This is good. If time allows you might let YouTube call up another video, and if you like that one you will let YouTube call up yet another video. As long as you're getting that rush of feeling pleasantly different at the end of each video than you did at the beginning you will let YouTube show you videos all day. You like YouTube. But what happens when YouTube serves you a video you don't like? One that bores you, or is uninteresting? You're out of here.

You feel irritated and frustrated and you close YouTube and move on. You no longer like YouTube. Your internet sales prospects react the same way to you and your outreaches; as long as they feel pleasantly better at the end of each email or voice message or text than they did when they started they will like you and your dealership. If not....

Additional notes:

- Many industry professionals advocate and employ email templates designed to guilt or shame the nonresponsive prospect into replying. (Example: "Is there a reason you have not returned my calls?" or "Have I done something wrong?" etc. etc.) To our mind, while the nagging spouse / nagging parent approach may work on prospects with reduced self-esteem, others will find the tone of the emails to be arrogant and audacious. In our opinion, displaying chutzpah is not the way to get the nonresponsive prospect to open up to you. Nevertheless, some stores report great success with this type of template. (We think it only works if the prospect is first pleased and impressed with the FQR email sent on Day 1. You may have a differing opinion).
- Consider this: Amazon.com, L.L. Bean, Home Depot and the hundreds of other companies who email you regularly have to impact you with email only – they can't call all 1,000,000+ people on their prospects list. They successfully write and send template-based emails that cause people to take a course of action. Why can't you? (You can).

Here's a challenge: when composing templates pretend that none of your e-prospects has provided a telephone number. You are now forced to create sales excitement solely through the written word. Can you give value, advance the sales momentum, and deliver your needed message in as few words as possible?

WHY DON'T THEY REPLY TO MY EMAILS?

Do you feel that your outbound emails should be generating more results? Pretty much everyone does.

It's tempting to blame prospects for being inconsiderate jerks. "Why do these people send in leads if they don't want to buy?" "These leads suck – these people are just shoppers!"

But as any professional stage performer knows, if the audience isn't applauding your act it's not because they don't want to be entertained. It's because you, the performer, are not in step with what they want to see and hear right now.

- Remember what we said earlier: today's Internet car shoppers are self-educating themselves as much as they can, contacting retailers only when it becomes a necessary step toward reaching their purchase goal. They expect you to provide value in the form of information that helps them advance themselves to the inevitable sale. No info of value = no engagement.

- One email no longer makes an impact. It's been a long time since people got excited every time their computer exclaimed "You've got mail!" Everyone receives hundreds of emails per day now with the majority of them junk or irrelevant. To stand out and register with the reader today you have to be relevant (i.e. give value) and you have to be in front of their eyes repeatedly. Email has become like billboards; how many times must you drive by the same billboard before it finally sticks in your head? A lot.

- Are your emails fugly? Are they too wordy? Are they too stuffy and formal sounding? People today expect stuff to be personal, concise, professional and easy on the eyes. *Do this: gather a sampling of your outbound emails and read them out loud. How do they sound? Upbeat and conversational? Or stilted and awkward? Crisp and concise? Or long and painful? Reading them out loud will reveal everything that is right or wrong about your email communications.*

It's often hard to evaluate the communications effectiveness of our own emails - we are just too close to the material to have an objective eye. However, you have an invaluable (and free) resource right under your nose – the wife! (Or husband. Or cousin. Or best friend. Or whatever.) One who is not in the car business. Who does not read car magazines. Who is only interested in cars for their ability to get them from point A to B, for their safety and their reliability. (And maybe their status). Sounds like an average tough customer, right?

If you have a spouse, or cousin or friend (or whatever), male or female, who is not in the car business *and is not impassioned about cars*, ask him/her to mystery shop your store and give you his/her subjective analysis. Ask them:
- "What first impression did you get when you saw this email/these emails?"
- "How did it make you feel after you read it?"
- "Was the information presented valuable to you?"
- "Was it easy to read and understand?"
- "Did this email make you like our dealership and/or the salesperson sending it?"

It beats paying money for an outside focus group. And you'll likely be startled by the results.

TELEPHONE: WHAT TO SAY

Easy Phone Script-less Solution
One common reason salespeople stop making follow-up phone calls is they don't know what to say. This is understandable; how many times can you leave this message "Hi _____, Tom here at ABC Motors, just wondering' if you're still interested in that Camry you asked about?" before you feel foolish or filled with dread at the pointlessness of it?

However, there is an easy and foolproof phone trick that solves the problem regardless of whether you get the answering machine or the prospect picks up the phone.

What to say when you call:

- Tell them that you just sent an email of value ("...and please let me know if you didn't get it.")
- Or, simply reiterate the message that is in the email you last sent. (Example: "Did you know it only takes 20 minutes to get a guaranteed appraisal at our store...?")

It's as simple as that. And it doesn't require any memorization or reading of words that sound canned or unnatural.

Example: On Day 1 send the FQR email first and then call. For a message all you have to do is say this: "Hi Joe, this is Bob at ABC Motors, I received your request and replied to it already. Check your email and please let me know if you cannot find it or do not have it." You just left a message that gave value to the customer!

Then on Day 2 – 5 (or however long you continue phone attempts) leave a message that matches the one in that day's follow-up email. Example: if on Day 2 you sent a Trade-In info email then on that same day leave a voice message that reiterates the email's message. "Hi Joe, this is Bob at ABC Motors. Do you have a car or truck to trade-in? Did you know it only takes 20 minutes to get a guaranteed appraisal at our store...?"

For days that follow just use the same procedure; leave a voice message that mimics the content of that day's value-giving outgoing email. (Note: if, for example, there is an email task on, say, Day 6 but no telephone call task until Day 7, no problem. Just leave a voice message that mimics the contents of the Day 6 email.)

If you follow this practice every voice message you deliver gives value to the customer and (therefore) advances the sales momentum.

Never again will you leave a message that says "Call me if you have any questions or concerns"! (More on this one on the next page.)

WHAT <u>NOT</u> TO SAY

Please promise us you will never, ever use these phrases in your email, phone or text outreaches to customers.

- "Hassle free"
- "Questions or concerns"`
- "Earn your business"

Our mystery shoppers encounter these tired and counter-productive phrases all the time in emails and voice messages. Please avoid them at all costs. Here's why:

Hassle Free – introduces a negative (hassle). One of the first rules in sales communication is never, ever introduce a negative because negatives introduce fear and fear destroys trust. When you say "I promise you a hassle free experience" the customer thinks "Why is he/she saying that? I wasn't expecting this shopping experience to be a 'hassle.' Should I be? Otherwise, why did he/she bring it up? I'm starting to get a little nervous...."

Questions Or Concerns – another one that introduces a negative (concern). People become concerned when they suspect things are taking a wrong turn. When you ask "Do you have any questions or concerns?" the customer thinks "Why is he/she saying that? *Should* I be having concerns?" More important, however, is that we see this phrase used over and over when it is clear that the salesperson has run out of things to say and doesn't know what to do next. It's lazy.

Earn Your Business – this phrase was already tired when we first heard it over twenty five year ago. As used in the car biz "What's it gonna take to earn your business?" almost inevitably means "Let's cut to the chase. What price are you telling me you want to buy this for? Name your offer." A seller truly *earns* a buyer's business through trust, transparency, good salesmanship and good value pricing. If, instead, we use it to mean "How cheap do you think I have to be to get you to buy?" we have merely capitulated to get the customer's attention. We haven't *earned* anything at all. "Earn your business" is a disingenuous phrase and consumers know it.

TEXT MESSAGE CONTENT

Texting (mobile device text messaging via Short Message System [SMS] protocol) is a relatively new mode of communication – a decade ago very few American cell phone users had text capability. In 2008 texting exploded, and today SMS text messaging is the most widely used data application in the world, with 2.4 billion active users, or 74% of all mobile phone subscribers. (And this is a 2013 statistic. It has to be higher now.)

As a general rule, text messages are brief (the original technology kept messages at 160 characters or less). They are also immediate; text messages arrive within seconds of being sent. Also, the fact that they appear only on your personal cell phone gives them an intimacy that email lacks.

Airlines text you when your flight is delayed. Restaurants text you when your table is ready. UPS texts you when your package is delivered. Uber texts you when you driver arrives. Car dealer service departments text you when your car is ready! Likewise, you can text your sales prospects with brief, immediate and personal messages of value.

Example - Day 1: Once a new eLead arrives send the FQR (first quality response) email, then place a phone call. Now text. Your message should be as short and simple as this:

> Hi Tom. Fred @ Acme Buick. Got your request, replied by email. Let me know if you do not receive. Let's set up a test drive. Thanks!

Casual, personal, short and to the point. And it gives value.

Example - Day 2:

> Hi Tom. Fred @ Acme Buick.
> Just sent you more info.
> Check your email. Thanks!

Note that text messaging must be used sparingly. Whereas most customers are comfortable letting you issue a deliberately paced stream of emails over a long term, they will not accept the same from text messaging, which, as we said, appears only on the recipient's personal phone and is much more difficult to ignore.

There is no established rule for how many text messages you should send to a nonresponsive prospect before giving up, though most people we talk to seem to agree that 1 or 2 is enough.

Note: not every eLead gives you a cell phone number. If you don't know if the prospect's phone # is a cell phone or not just go to www.whitepages.com/reverse_phone and find out. Or just text anyway and see what happens. If the number they gave you is a land line the text will bounce and you will know immediately.

Some CRMs allow you to send texts directly from your computer keyboard. This is a great feature for two reasons: 1). It's much faster and easier to type your text message from a full sized computer keyboard than from a smart phone, and 2). If you send your text from within your CRM you now have a copy of record in the prospect's profile.

If your CRM does not have a text messaging feature there are numerous web vendors that enable you to send text messages from your PC via a browser. www.joopz.com, www.bulletin.net, and www.google.com/voice (Google Voice) are just a few. Check 'em out.

USING TARGETED BULK (BLAST) EMAIL

When done correctly, bulk email is an extremely effective way to generate quick traffic boosts to your store. Bulk email is fast, it's easy to do and, best of all it's free. What possible reason is there for not using bulk email at your store?

The goal of a bulk email is to help unsold and/or unresponsive prospects advance themselves from Gatherers to Sorters. Therefore, every outgoing bulk email should contain a strong call to action. *Use bulk emails to sell.*

If you are using your CRM to automatically send regular long term follow-up messages to unsold and/or unresponsive prospects every 7 – 10 days then 1 or 2 bulk emails each month is likely all you need.

Alternatively, some dealerships use bulk email as their only long term email follow-up Process and this is fine; if your store sends out a bulk email once every 7 – 10 days you are making enough regular "touches" to stay in front of the unsold and/or unresponsive prospects in your CRM database.

BULK EMAIL CONTENT: Many dealers use bulk email to send electronic versions of their print "box ads" and there is certainly no harm in getting double use out of a print graphic. However, it's worth noting that print advertising is usually designed to shower a broad common denominator audience, whereas email marketing is more effective when recipients are made to feel that they are part of a niche audience (i.e. "targeted"). Also, print car ads tend to "shout" at people, and whereas that captures attention to the printed page it can be abrasive on a screen. The best email marketing pieces tend to be quieter and more personal than broadcast print pieces.

Ultimately, there are no hard and fast rules as to what makes a great bulk email template or bulk email campaign. Experiment a bit until you find what works best for your store.

In the two examples here we show proven effective bulk email templates with strong calls to action that, nevertheless, are quieter and more personal than your typical car dealer email.

Example # 1: DOWN TO OUR LAST FEW SALE – bulk email. It's an age-old truism that the best way to get people to want something is to tell them they can't have it. In the email example below we tell the recipients that we have an outstanding sale, but only a limited amount of merchandise – this is a time-tested approach that has worked for centuries.

The small quantity of product made available (5 - 10 units seems to work best) gives the offer an air of exclusivity that appeals to people looking for a "special deal." Notice that the merchandise is described in such a way that the interested prospect has to contact the store in order to learn which vehicles have what specific trim lines and colors. This is the opposite of the tact used in most car ads, in which everything about the product is revealed up front. Here we create mystery by withholding some product details.

We have discovered that this template can be used across all prospects in your database and need not be filtered for new (versus used vehicles of interest) or model-specific prospects only. Send it to everyone. This email has generated responses from prospects not at all interested in the make and model being promoted who nevertheless are so intrigued by the approach that they ask if the store has sale pricing on the year, make and model vehicle in which they do have interest.

You can write variations on this template concept and use it to sell aged inventory, to sell a small inventory of multiple model vehicles, to sell used cars, or just about anything else for which you can create a perceived scarcity. (The example next uses Ford F-150 as the promoted vehicle).

SUBJECT LINE: Are You A Bargain Hunter? Few Remaining 2016
F-150s Deep Discounted Now

Tommy Carguy
Internet Sales
709-709-0709 cell

FRIENDLY MOTORS

Your Friends In The Car Business! Since 1983.
709 W Loop Hwy - Eddyville TX 70909   709-709-7090

Hi <{CustFirstName}>–

We have only five new 2016 F-150s remaining in stock - and they
are deep discounted right now!

Four are 4 X 2 Super Cabs, one is a 4 X 4 Super Crew.

One is an XLT, three are STX, and one is a Lariat Platinum.

Colors are Tuxedo Black, Blue Flame, Vermillion Red, and Royal
Red.

With all combined rebates/incentives & Ford Motor financing you
can drive away in one of these trucks for as low as $XX,XXX (+
TT&L).*

These are not demos! These are new and unsold trucks ready for a
good home.

But we've only got five - and when they're gone, they're gone.

Ready for your test drive? Call or write me today!

<{EmailSignature}>

*Dealer: be sure you are in compliance with your state and local laws regarding motor
vehicle advertising price and discount claims.*

Example # 2: MAY I RE-PRICE YOUR QUOTE? – Bulk email.
(With thanks to Ford Digital Team mate Jason Robinson for coming up with this one).
This template capitalizes upon the fact that manufacturers announce new retail incentives sometime after the first of each month. Most CRMs will allow you to write a bulk email campaign with criteria filters. In this case, the filters will be "Desired Vehicle = New" and "Prospect Created Date = (all dates prior to the date new incentives began this month)."

You can get double use out of this template by including it in your CRM automated emails long term follow-up Process. Set up the Process so this template goes out after the 6th or 7th of each month, or, if your Process is timeline-based, set it up so this template is used when a prospect is 35 or more days old (so that they assuredly arrived when the previous month's incentives were in place) and every 30-40 days or so thereafter. (Using the 180 Process provided earlier in this chapter, you can make this template the Day 40, 70, 110, and 150 template).

Hi <{CustFirstName}>,

It's been a few weeks now since you sent me your request. Our inventory, store promotions, and factory incentives have changed.

The <{SoughtMake}> <{SoughtModel}> sale price offer I sent you is no longer current. Can I send you a new price today?

Just reply to this letter – and let me know what you are now looking for. I'll get back to you with a new price and anything else you want.

<{EmailSignature}>

MAKE YOUR TEMPLATES SMART-PHONE-FRIENDLY

The biggest change in electronic communications in the past couple years has been the explosive growth of smart phones.

- 92% of all Americans now have cell phones – and all but 24% of those are smart phones. (And this was as of 2015. Has to be a much smaller % now.)
- Up to 40% of all emails are now read on smart phones only.
- 67% of consumers say they check their email on their mobile phone.
- 80% of consumers say they delete an email on their mobile phone if it doesn't look good. (Up from 69.7% in 2012).

In the Dallas, TX market area (where I work) it is not unusual for dealership website analytics to reveal that more than 50% of all visitors to a dealer's website get there on a smart phone or tablet. All of the information above means that your CRM email templates must be sized and formatted to look good and be readable on a smart phone. How do your templates look on smart phones? Send them to yourself to find out.

Here are some general guidelines to follow when composing your templates:

- Limit graphic headers to around 500 pixels in width.
- Avoid using frames and/or tables in the header. (Some brand CRM templates are formatted this way right out of the box. Delete them).
- Avoid sidebars (side frames or side tables) at all cost.
- Do not frame (surround) the content field (main text area).
- Do not paste large images (i.e. window stickers, big newspaper ad image files, etc.) into the body (main text area). (Note that one vehicle photo will usually size just fine)
- Keep content (text) to a minimum; make the message short and sweet.

- Suggestion: put your store's phone number in the subject line of the emails. On smart phones the phone number reads as a hyperlink; the user hits it once with his/her thumb and the phone calls your store.

ADDITIONAL NOTE ON GRAPHIC HEADERS

Studies have proven that while the public likes and trusts car manufacturers, they do not like and trust car dealers. You can work this to a competitive advantage when creating a graphic header for your outgoing emails. At the beginning of each month, when your brand's OEM launches its current promotion, update your graphic header to copy the images, slogans and overall "look" of that promotion. In this way, your outgoing emails mimic the appearance of OEM outgoing material. When customers see your emails they now view your store as an adjunct of the manufacturer and are more inclined to trust you and the dealership. (Conversely, the dealer who seeks to distance himself from the manufacturer and create his own public persona can actually increase the public's distrust of his dealership).

GOOD TEMPLATE EXAMPLES

We are in no way suggesting that these are the best and only templates a dealership can use. They are provided here as examples of email templates that we have found, been given, or created and that are known to work, today or in the recent past. Some may be appropriate for your store, some may not. The one constant in every template is that they always give value. Feel free to utilize (or not utilize) them anyway you see fit.

Note that the merge codes shown in these examples work with the eLeads brand CRM. If you copy these templates you will need to insert the merge codes appropriate to your store's brand CRM.

#1 AUTORESPONDER

SUBJECT LINE: Friendly Motors Received Your Request

Hi <{CustFirstName}> -

Thank you for asking <{DealershipName}> to help you find your next car or truck!

We will return promptly during business hours with the information you requested.

We look forward to talking to you soon.

<{EmailSignature}>

This autoresponse template is intentionally short and to the point. An autoresponder should be a receipt, nothing more. "We got your request, we're on the case, back at ya soon." *That's it.* Save the selling and informing for later.

#2 FQR – NEW CAR or TRUCK – GENERAL INQUIRY
SUBJECT LINE: [Vehicle Year, Make & Model] From Friendly
Motors (709) 709-7090

Hi <{CustFirstName}> -

Good news! We have <{SoughtModel}> models in stock right now for you
to see and drive.

Do you like this one? It is available and on sale:

INSERT VEHICLE PHOTO HERE

<{SoughtYear}> <{SoughtMake}> <{SoughtModel}>   Stock #
Exterior color   / Interior color .
Key options/upgrades/packages:
MSRP +$
Current factory-to-consumer discount/rebate incentives* -$
<{DealershipName}> special discount -$
Your <{DealershipName}> sale price = $ (+ TT&L).

Did you know? <{SoughtMake}> is offering __% financing or $___mo.
lease special on this model too. This ends soon!

You can have a free, no obligation <{SoughtMake}> <{SoughtModel}> test
drive today. Shall we make an appointment now? Or can I bring one by
your home or workplace today instead?

I'll call you in a little bit to be sure you got this email.

<{EmailSignature}>

*Some factory-to-consumer incentives are contingent upon having a trade-in vehicle and/or
using manufacturer-provided financing. Special **additional discounts** and/or incentives may
also be available to you as a qualified buyer. I will work to be sure you receive all the
discounts and incentives for which you are eligible!*

#3 FQR – NEW CAR or TRUCK – GEN INQUIRY w/ SPECS
SUBJECT LINE: [Vehicle Year, Make & Model] From Friendly Motors (709) 709-7090

Hi <{CustFirstName}> -

You are in luck! I have a <{SoughtModel}> just like the one you specified - **OR** - I have a <{SoughtModel}> much like the one you specified - **OR** - I have located a <{SoughtModel}> like the one you specified.

Have you driven a <{SoughtModel}> yet? I have this one we can test drive to see how you like them.

INSERT VEHICLE PHOTO

<{SoughtYear}> <{SoughtMake}> <{SoughtModel}>   Stock #
Exterior color   / Interior color .
Key options/upgrades/packages:
MSRP +$
Current factory-to-consumer discount/rebate incentives* -$
<{DealershipName}> special discount -$
Your <{DealershipName}> sale price = $ (+ TT&L).

Did you know? <{SoughtMake}> is offering __% financing or $___mo. lease special on this model too. This ends soon!

I'll call you in a little bit to be sure you got this email.

Talk to you soon.

<{EmailSignature}>

*Some factory-to-consumer incentives are contingent upon having a trade-in vehicle and/or using manufacturer-provided financing. Special **additional discounts** and/or incentives may also be available to you as a qualified buyer. I will work to be sure you receive all the discounts and incentives for which you are eligible!*

#4 FQR – NEW CAR or TRUCK – IN-STOCK UNIT (VIN specific)
SUBJECT LINE: [Vehicle Year, Make & Model] From Friendly
Motors (709) 709-7090

Hi <{CustFirstName}> -

Good news! The <{SoughtYear}> <{SoughtMake}> <{SoughtModel}> you
like, stock #<{SoughtStockNum}>, is here and ready for you to see and
test drive.

INSERT VEHICLE PHOTO HERE

<{SoughtYear}> <{SoughtMake}> <{SoughtModel}>
VIN #<{SoughtVin}>
Exterior color   / Interior color   .
Key options/upgrades/packages:
MSRP +$
Current factory discounts/rebates/incentives* -$
<{DealershipName}> special discount -$
Your <{DealershipName}> sale price = $ (+ TT&L).

Did you know? <{SoughtMake}> is offering __% financing or $___mo.
lease special on this model too. Ends soon!

You can have a free, no obligation test drive of this <{SoughtModel}>
today. Shall we make an appointment now? Or can I bring it by your home
or workplace today instead?

I'll call you in a little bit to be sure you got this email.

<{EmailSignature}>

** Some factory-to-consumer incentives are contingent upon having a trade-in vehicle and/or
using manufacturer-provided financing. Special **additional discounts** and/or incentives may
also be available to you as a qualified buyer. I will work to be sure you receive all the
discounts and incentives for which you are eligible!*

#5 FQR – USED CAR or TRUCK – IN-STOCK UNIT
SUBJECT LINE: [Vehicle Year, Make & Model] From Friendly
Motors (709) 709-7090

Tommy Carguy
Internet Sales
709-709-0709 cell

Hi <{CustFirstName}> -

Good news! The <{SoughtYear}> <{SoughtMake}>
<{SoughtModel}> you like, stock #<{SoughtStockNum}>, is here
and ready for you to see and drive.

INSERT VEHICLE PHOTO HERE

<{SoughtYear}> <{SoughtMake}> <{SoughtModel}>
VIN # <{SoughtVin}>
Exterior color   / Interior color
Key options/upgrades/packages:
Kelly Blue Book values this vehicle at $
Your <{DealershipName}> special sale price is $!(+ TT&L)

<{DealershipName}> has low rate installment financing and
extended service agreements for this vehicle too.

You can have a free, no obligation test drive of this
<{SoughtModel}> today. Shall we make an appointment now? Or
can I bring it by your home or workplace today instead?

I'll call you in a little bit to be sure you got this email.

Talk to you soon.

<{EmailSignature}>

#6 FQR – TRADE-IN VALUATION LEAD

SUBJECT LINE: Here's More About Your Trade-In Value - Friendly Motors (709) 709-7090

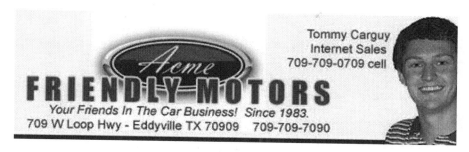

Hi <{CustFirstName}> -

Thank you for using our online Trade-In Value Estimator!

The numbers you saw are "sight unseen" estimates and therefore general.

Want a firm number? Just let our appraisers check out your vehicle in person. We will give you a Guaranteed Trade-In Offer while you wait.

A free, no obligation market value appraisal at our dealership takes just 20 minutes.

I'll help you look up your loan or lease payoff while you wait, too.

Or you can test drive that <{SoughtYear}> <{SoughtMake}> <{SoughtModel}> you have your eye on.

You can make an appointment now – my contact info appears below.

I'll call you in a little bit to be sure you got this email.

Talk to you soon.

<{EmailSignature}>

#7 FQR – COLD CREDIT APP LEAD
SUBJECT LINE: Friendly Motors Received Your Financing Request

Hi <{CustFirstName}> -

Thank you for your credit inquiry.

Please allow me to look it over. If there is any missing info I'll be sure to call you right away.

Once I know the application is complete I'll review it with our Finance Office, then call you to discuss in confidence.

<{EmailSignature}>

#8 SEND @ END 1ST DAY IF CUSTOMER UNRESPONSIVE
SUBJECT LINE: Did You Get Your Reply From Friendly Motors? (709) 709-7090

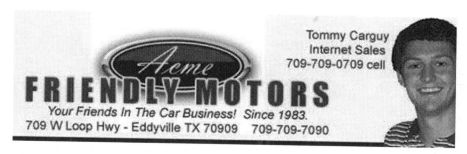

Hi <{CustFirstName}> -

I got your request and replied right away. Did you get it?

Did I send what you're looking for?

Please let me know. Thanks!

<{EmailSignature}>

#9 TRADE-IN LETTER (Send 2nd day if customer unresponsive)
SUBJECT LINE: What About The Car Or Truck You Have Now?

Hi <{CustFirstName}>,

Are you thinking of selling your current car or truck? If so, can we see it?

A free, no obligation market value appraisal at our store takes just 20 minutes.

I'll help you look up your loan or lease payoff while you wait, too.

Or you can test drive that <{SoughtYear}> <{SoughtMake}> <{SoughtModel}> you have your eye on.

It's easy to make an appointment – my contact info appears below.

I'll also call you in a little bit to be sure you received this email.

Thanks.

<{EmailSignature}>

#10 FINANCE LETTER (Send 3rd day if customer unresponsive)
SUBJECT LINE: Save Time – Finance In Advance At Friendly
Motors (709) 709-7090

Hi <{CustFirstName}>,

You can save time and do a lot of your paperwork details BEFORE
you come here for a test drive.

Like financing. Click **HERE,** complete the short and simple
application, then "Submit."

Your new wheels might be just a mouse click away!

<{EmailSignature}>

++ *INSTALLER: make "HERE" a hyperlink to dealer's website's
credit app page.*

#11 I'LL KEEP TRYING (Send 4th day if customer unresponsive)
SUBJECT LINE: I'll Keep Trying. (Friendly Motors 709-709-7090)

Hi <{CustFirstName}>,

Sorry we've been unable to connect. But I'll keep trying!

Is it possible you're already talking to someone else at our store?

Or should I be reaching you a better way?

What do you like best? Email? Phone? Text?

Just say the word.

Thanks.

<{EmailSignature}>

#12 LET US COME TO YOU (Send 5th day if customer unresponsive)
SUBJECT LINE: Can't Come Here? We'll Come To You

Hi <{CustFirstName}>,

If it's hard for you to visit our store let me bring a car or truck to you.

I can meet you at your home or workplace* at a day and time when it is convenient. It's all part of the service.

Ready to make an appointment? My contact info is below. I look forward to hearing from you.

<{EmailSignature}>

* Within a reasonable distance from our store, of course.

#13 LETTER FROM THE MANAGER (Send 6th day if customer still unresponsive. We recommend letting the CRM send this and all subsequent emails automatically.)

SUBJECT LINE: How Are We Doing? Friendly Motors Really Wants Your Opinion

Hi <{CustFirstName}>,

I'm <{GeneralManagerFullName}>, General Manager of <{DealershipName}>.

I'd really like to know what you think of your Internet car shopping experience so far. How are we doing?

- Did we send you a nice price on the <{SoughtMake}> <{SoughtModel}> you want?
- Are you getting the additional assistance you want?
- Is there anything we can do to make getting a car or truck easier for you?

If you are delighted with our service so far I'd love to know.

If you are not delighted with our service I NEED to know.

My contact information appears below. Please take a moment to tell me what you think. I truly appreciate it.

Thanks in advance.

<{GeneralManagerFullName}>
<{DealershipName}>
<{DealershipEmail}>
<{DealershipPhone}>

#14 CONSUMER REVIEWS LETTER

SUBJECT LINE: What Do Our Customers Say About
<{DealershipName}>?

Hi <{CustFirstName}> -

We don't need to talk about our great customer service – our
customers do it for us!

Link to reviews page here

When people like their <{SoughtMake}> dealer word gets around;
<{DealershipName}> has been a Top 100 and _____ Award
<{SoughtMake}> dealer __ times.

At <{DealershipName}> we've got great people, great service, and
the most exciting vehicles on the market today.   Let us show you!

<{EmailSignature}>

#15 YOU NAME IT WE CAN GET IT
SUBJECT LINE: You Name It We Can Get It

Hi <{CustFirstName}>,

I have access to thousands of new <{SoughtMake}> vehicles through the <{SoughtMake}> dealer network.

If the car or truck you want has been built, I can find it.

OR - if we can't find one exactly like you want why not factory order?

There is no additional charge to have one built just for you.

Locate or order? The choice is yours. Please just call or write and describe what you want. I'll start looking right away!

<{EmailSignature}>

#16 NOBODY LIKES TO BE SOLD
SUBJECT LINE: Nobody Likes To Be Sold.

Hi <{CustFirstName}> -

They say everybody likes to buy, but nobody likes to be sold.

At <{DealershipName}> we don't want to <u>sell</u> you anything. Instead, we want to <u>help</u> you get to where you want to be.

We've got great people, great service, and the best cars and trucks on the market today.

Let me show you!

<{EmailSignature}>

#17 BARGAIN HUNTER
SUBJECT LINE: Are You A Bargain Hunter?

Hi <{CustFirstName}> -

Need some cheap wheels? Then check out the Bargain Lot at
<{DealershipName}>.

These are great used vehicles that, for whatever reason, have
simply been in our inventory too long. Before we wholesale them to
other dealers you've got a shot at grabbing one yourself at a near-
wholesale price.

Everybody loves a bargain. But bargains don't last. Check out
<{DealershipName}>'s Bargain Lot today then contact me for a test
drive appointment!

<{EmailSignature}>

#18 THE FIRST ONE'S FREE
SUBJECT LINE: The First One's On The House

Hi <{CustFirstName}> -

The day you buy a new car or truck from us is a happy day.

But we want to be sure you stay happy after the sale too.

That's why at <{DealershipName}> your first scheduled new vehicle maintenance visit is on us.

That's right – free. Gratis. Comped.

It's our little way of checking back to make sure you are delighted with your purchase.

Will we be seeing you soon?

<{EmailSignature}>

#19 CPO MEANS PEACE OF MIND
SUBJECT LINE: Certified Pre-Owned Means Peace Of Mind

Tommy Carguy
Internet Sales
709-709-0709 cell

FRIENDLY MOTORS
Acme
Your Friends In The Car Business! Since 1983.
709 W Loop Hwy - Eddyville TX 70909   709-709-7090

Hi <{CustFirstName}> -

How would you like to purchase a just-like-new car or truck - but - for a less than new car or truck price? You can with <{DealershipName}>'s Certified Pre-Owned (CPO) cars program.

Every Certified Pre-Owned <{SoughtMake}> has passed a stringent 172 point mechanical inspection and comes with a free CARFAX® Vehicle History Report™

PLUS - every <{SoughtMake}> Certified Pre-Owned vehicle comes with a comprehensive limited warranty covering more than 500 components for 12 months/12,000 miles.

PLUS - you get 7-year/100,000-mile powertrain limited warranty coverage and free 24 hour Roadside Assistance.

PLUS - you get <{SoughtMake}> financing as low as 1.9% APR.
(With approved credit of course).

If you have not already considered a Certified Pre-Owned <{SoughtMake}> check out our current selection!

You might drive home with more car for less money than you were planning to spend.

What's not to like about that?

<{EmailSignature}>

#20 IT'S ALL ABOUT YOU
SUBJECT LINE: It's All About You

Hi <{CustFirstName}>,

Just want you to know that if you need time I am patient.

And if you need help but are afraid to ask, don't be. Just ask me.

I don't care whether you are in the early information gathering stage
or you are ready to buy now, I will give you the same amount of
attention.

May we be your dealership?

<{EmailSignature}>

#21 CHALLENGE US
SUBJECT LINE: We Like To Be Challenged

Hi <{CustFirstName}>,

I like to solve problems.

Is there an obstacle keeping you from buying the new ride you want?

Let me try to make that obstacle go away.

Please write or call and let me know what's standing between you and the car or truck you want.

I look forward to the challenge!

<{EmailSignature}>

THE GOOD, THE BAD, AND THE UGLY: DECONSTRUCTING DEALER EMAILS

In this section we are going to dissect and analyze some actual emails received over the past few years by our mystery shoppers.

1). THE AUTO-RESPONSE

Dear James Smith,

Thank you for your request on the 2015 Volkswagen Jetta. I am pleased that you have considered Friendly Motors *(not the dealer's real name)* to assist you and your family with your present or future automotive needs.

I want to make sure that your request is processed properly and that your internet experience is an enjoyable one.

It will be my pleasure to assist you in purchasing your new vehicle. Please be patient while specific vehicle details are gathered and a search for the vehicle to match your request is made.

If you would like to see our monthly specials or in stock vehicles, please visit our website at **www.friendlymotors.com**.

Friendly Motors offers all clients a comprehensive program of amenities and privileges which include:
- Complimentary Shuttle Transportation
- Complimentary Car Washes during Business Hours
- Client Lounges with Wireless Internet Access Hi-Definition Flat Screen TV's
- Complimentary Beverages
- Online Service Scheduling and Convenient Saturday Hours

Looking forward to speaking with you and thank you for contacting Friendly Motors.

Proud member of the Friendly Motors Auto Group.

Tommy Salesman

OK, what is wrong with this letter? Other than everything? Let's examine it line by line:

Dear James Smith,

"Dear First Name Last Name" seems terribly formal, no? Formalities are conducted at arm's length – they reduce emotional connection, not increase it. Why are we passing on the opportunity to establish an immediate emotional connection with him? Wouldn't *"Hi James"* be much more friendly and inviting?

Thank you for your request on the 2015 Volkswagen Jetta.

We haven't completed the first sentence and already something feels wrong. The word "on" isn't right, causing the whole line to seem clumsy and awkward. How about *"Thank you for asking us about the 2015 Volkswagen Jetta"*? Isn't that simpler and friendlier?

I am pleased that you have considered Friendly Motors to assist you and your family with your present or future automotive needs.

Why is this paragraph even in here?
* You already thanked the prospect in the previous line - why does he care that you are pleased?
* The lead was sent in by one person – why do you mention family? How do you know he has family or that they are in any way involved in this purchase?
* Why do you mention *future* needs? You want him to buy a car today, not in the future. Why is this distraction in here?
* Overall, the sentence is too long - and passive. It has no energy at all. Try this instead: *"Thank you for asking Friendly Motors to help you find your next car or truck!"* We just condensed 23 words into 15 and gave the sentence much more energy and immediacy.

* "...pleased" is a past tense word (ends in "ed") whereas "Thank you" takes place in the present. The present always has more energy and excitement.

    * "...you have considered" is past tense and long (five syllables) whereas "asking" takes place in the present (ends in "ing") and has only two syllables.

I want to make sure that your request is processed properly and that your internet experience is an enjoyable one.

OK, that's nice and all but, really, WHO CARES? Can we please get past these introductory remarks? You are all talk and no action. We're getting pretty bored, buddy. Keep it moving! Delete this paragraph.

It will be my pleasure to assist you in purchasing your new vehicle.

Haven't you now told the prospect <u>three times</u> that you appreciate him and want to please him? Why is this here? Strike it!

Please be patient while specific vehicle details are gathered and a search for the vehicle to match your request is made.

* "Please be patient..."!?!? So at this early stage of the relationship, and having already bored us to death, you are now telling us to go sit down and wait? This is the Internet, man, we want instant answers now!

* "...while specific vehicle details are gathered and a search for the vehicle to match your request is made." You mean, like, you need some big Univac computer to collect his specific vehicle details (didn't he just give you those in his inquiry?) and next you need to comb the earth to find a car like the one he requested? Aren't you a new car dealership? Isn't that why he chose you? Aren't you supposed to have these things in stock? WTH?

Can we please try this instead? *"I will reply promptly with the exact information you requested."* Hello! Thank you! That's all we're looking for. We also just condensed 21 words into 10. The new sentence is quicker, cleaner and far more energetic.

If you would like to see our monthly specials or in stock vehicles, please visit our website at **www.friendlymotors.com**.

Okay…why is this here? Who said anything about monthly specials? We're still waiting for the info that was requested. Now you've gone off topic and changed the subject of the letter! Plus, by directing us to your website, you are effectively telling the prospect to go back out into the store and shop some more. He's standing at your cash register with year/make/model merchandise he selected (he submitted a lead, remember?) and you are telling him to go back out and wander around in the store some more. Why in the world would you want to do that?

Friendly Motors offers all clients a comprehensive program of amenities and privileges which include:
- Complimentary Shuttle Transportation
- Complimentary Car Washes during Business Hours
- Client Lounges with Wireless Internet Access & Hi-Definition Flat Screen TV's
- Complimentary Beverages
- Online Service Scheduling and Convenient Saturday Hours

Sigh Sure, this is nice and all but, once again, you've changed the subject. One letter = one topic. The purpose of this letter is not to sell us on the dealership. (That comes later.) This is an autoresponder: it should be nothing more than an acknowledgement that you received the lead. So far you have told us that we are appreciated (three times), then told us to be patient while you search the planet for a car, then told us to go back out in the store and shop. And now you tell us about your store's amenities. MEANWHILE – we're still waiting for info – and beginning to suspect that it's never going to arrive. Kill this whole section, please.

Looking forward to speaking with you and thank you for contacting Friendly Motors.

Not only is this an incomplete sentence, but it also tries to say two things in one sentence. (Looking forward to speaking + thank you.) Remember: one sentence = one thought.   Suggest instead: *"Thank you again for contacting Friendly Ford. I look forward to replying soon with the info you requested."* Drive home that you are the salesperson who is going to give him what he asked for!

Proud member of the Friendly Motors Auto Group.

Um, sure, whatever. It's another incomplete sentence but at this point we're too weary to care.

All we really need and want to do with the 1st automated response letter is tell the customer

- I/we got your request
- I'm on the case
- I'll be back soon with the goods.

That's it! If you want to say more say it in another email. We repeat again: one email = one topic.

By taking a surgical knife to this 2015 Jetta example we end up with a better autoresponse email reading something like this:

> Hi James -
>
> Thank you for asking Friendly Motors to help you find your next car or truck!
>
> We will return promptly during business hours with the information you requested.
>
> We look forward to talking to you soon.
>
> Tommy Salesman

Short, sweet, and on target.

2). THE ALL-CUSTOM NON-TEMPLATE FQR

Many Internet salespeople and sales managers are opposed to using templates for FQR emails (or any emails for that matter) thinking that they are too impersonal and robotic. Or that salespeople get lazy and, without reading the lead, just pick a template and hit "send" without really thinking about what they are sending. It's a good point, and one reason we have stressed on these pages the importance of reading the lead before using a template-based FQR. So why not delete all templates and let your people write custom FQRs every time?

Because they will forget to sell the car.

We see this all the time in our mystery shop adventures; personally written FQRs that fail the FQR Rater score sheet. (See "FQR Rater" earlier in the book.)

In the examples below our shopper selected an end-of-model-year F-150 from the dealers' inventories and in the "Comments" box wrote "Current incentives?"

Now let's look below at two real life examples from the extreme ends of the spectrum.

Dealer Number One:

> Dear James,
>
> I received your request for information on a 2015 Ford F-150. I tried to reach you by phone, so I could get a little more information from you and what we are trying to do. I can be reached by email or phone to better assist you at 000-000-0000 or tommys@friendlymotors.com.
>
> Tommy Salesman

"I tried to reach you by phone..." Can't argue this one – he is giving value by letting the customer know that he made an outreach attempt.

"...so I could get a little more information from you and what we are trying to do." ...and what we are trying to do? Huh? We assume he meant "...so I can get a little more information from you *and understand what you are trying to accomplish.*" That would have been great!

Remember when you get a lead you don't know

- Where they are in the shopping process. (Gatherer? Sorter? High funnel? Mid-funnel? Low funnel?)
- What they are trying to accomplish with this purchase.

Once you know the answer to those two questions you are well on your way to being able to sell the customer. But, sadly, this salesman typo'd the most important sentence in his FQR and came off looking somewhat sloppy. Bummer! This, of course, would not have happened had he used a template.

But that's a minor point: the salesman ultimately failed because he never gave the prospect the remaining key FQR components needed to educate and advance the consumer to the inevitable sale, components that would have been in his FQR template:

- Confirmation of the availability of product
- Merchandising the product (photo and description)
- Making an offer to sell something
- Letting the customer know that you will be advancing the sales momentum

Plus, this shopper never heard from this salesman again. ☹

His closing line, "I can be reached by email or phone to better assist you at..." is also a fail because he is throwing the sales momentum back into the customer's lap and saying "Tag, you're it!" Remember that the consumer has spent some time already on the Internet getting to the point where he wants/needs to submit a lead. Having done so it is now the salesperson's duty to pick up the ball and take it down the field. This salesman did not pick up and run the ball, nor did he provide the customer with the information the customer requested.

Score = 0.

Dealer Number Two:
On the other side of the scale is this far superior FQR we received from another dealer

Dear James,

Thank you for your inquiry. My name is Tommy Salesman, I'm the internet sales manager for Friendly Motors. I would like to be your sales person and help you from point A to Z with your purchase.

I see that you're in the market for a new 2015 F150 and would like to know about current incentives. The rebates right now are very high on the remaining 2015's available. The 2016's will be out in December or January so now is the best time to get the best deal on a 2015. The rebates depend on what cab size and series you're interested in.

The super cab 4x2 STX F150 that you inquired about is available and its window sticker is pasted below my contact info. This truck has $XXXX in total rebates available and an additional $XXXX rebate if you trade in a 1995 or newer vehicle making it $XXXX.

VEHICLE PHOTO HERE

However I would provide you with more discounts then this even. The supercab STX below MSRP's at $XXXXX but your sale price after all rebates (including financing with Ford and the additional trade-in rebate) would be $XXXXX!!

VEHICLE PHOTO HERE

This is really cutting to the chase and I can only offer this until the end of the month because the extra $XXXX trade-in rebate will go away on the 2nd of November.

However If you would be interested in a crewcab XLT then there is a total of $XXXX in rebates plus the trade-in rebate making the total $XXXX before my discounts.

Feel free to call or email me at any time. Thanks again for the inquiry and I look forward to hearing back from you soon.

Tommy Salesman

Wow! This guy is great! As a potential buyer I now feel totally informed, educated and illuminated. He just removed all the mystery and obfuscation surrounding pricing and incentives. He merchandized the product and made an offer to sell on not one but two new trucks. He made me feel that he is really looking out for me and wants to guide me to a smart, satisfying purchase. I trust him and I am ready to put myself into his hands. A beautiful piece of work, really. So what's the problem?

He forgot to ask for the appointment.

He ends with the dreaded "Feel free to call me any time" line which essentially releases the shopper from having any obligation to further the relationship with the salesman or his store. (By telling the shopper to feel free to call him it means there is no obligation, therefore the shopper is also free to not call him.) Had he used a proper template (or been able to discipline himself to always end his FQRs by advancing the sales momentum) this never would have happened.

Had he instead ended with "I will be calling you soon to be sure you got this email" or "I will be calling you soon to set up your test drive appointment" the shopper would have been on high alert and welcoming his call - especially if he had also followed the email with a text. ("Tommy @ Friendly Motors here. Got your request, replied via email. Will call soon to be sure you got.")

And, sadly, this shopper never heard from this salesman again. ☹

3). THE "BUY OR DIE" EMAIL
Here's something that was mentioned earlier and that we see a lot in mystery shops. It's an email (template in most cases) used by many dealers and one that we also used for a time when we were selling. We thought it was pretty good at the time but now that we're on the other side we feel differently. What do you think?

The letter in question always contains some variation of the following:

> Dear James –
>
> I received a request for a Camry from you several days ago. I have replied via email and phone, but, to date, I have gotten no response from you. Are you still in the market for a car?
>
> Perhaps you have not had time to answer my e-mail or phone calls regarding your vehicle purchase request. It is very important that I speak with you.

Some versions even go so far as to add:

> If you are no longer in the market just reply to this letter with 'Unsubscribe' in the subject line and I will remove you from my list.

We used to like this template because we felt that it flushed out the serious people and separated them from the window shoppers. Maybe so, but at what cost? The data proves that a great many Internet car shoppers contact dealers weeks, or even months, in advance of their actual buy date. Many like to lurk in the shadows, quietly gathering and processing information until they are ready to come out into the daylight. (Gatherers advancing themselves to become Sorters.)

Today, when our mystery shopper gets the "Are you still in the market?" letter we find ourself feeling that this dealer is only interested in us if we are ready to buy right now. And if we are not ready to buy right now any additional help we receive will be given begrudgingly.

Perhaps the most disturbing line is "It is very important that I talk to you." Really? And you are...who? The police? The IRS? The authorities? This line strikes us as being insolent.

The last line, "If you are no longer in the market just reply to this letter with 'Unsubscribe' in the subject line...," provides the only information of value in the email as by this point we are only too happy to oblige and opt out.

Is the "Are you still in the market" template a smart ploy? Or is it killing lurker gatherers and therefore killing potential future customers?

4). THE ZOMBIE FQR TEMPLATE

Remember that when you sign up for a CRM it comes pre-populated with a rudimentary sales process and a bunch of 25 year old templates that were bad when they were new. Because dealers switch CRMs all the time these templates keep resurfacing, refusing to die. Here's one zombie FQR our shopper received a couple years ago. Let's deconstruct it.

> Dear James,
>
> Thank you for your inquiry on the Subaru Outback. We currently have a great selection of Outbacks in stock starting as low as $00,000.00.
>
> To ensure I provide you with a price on a vehicle that meets your needs, it's important that I speak with you to determine which options and equipment are most important to you.
>
> I've enclosed an e-brochure for your convenience.
>
> I will be following up this email with a phone call so that we can discuss you specific needs.
>
> Thank you again for your inquiry and I look forward to speaking with you and for the opportunity to earn your business!
>
> Sincerely,
>
> Tommy Salesman

Now the breakdown and analysis:

> Thank you for your inquiry on the Subaru Outback. We currently have a great selection of Outbacks in stock starting as low as $00,000.00.

Score! He leads off with a confirmation of availability of the product. Plus he follows it with "…starting as low as $00,000" which can easily be construed as an offer to sell. So far so good.

> **To ensure I provide you with a price on a vehicle that meets your needs, it's important that I speak with you to determine which options and equipment are most important to you.**

And now we start to go off the rails.

- To begin we don't like the use of the word "needs." The shopper submitted a lead on an Outback – doesn't that mean he already thinks an Outback is a car that will meet his needs? It may or may not, but until he gets to your dealership you can't know whether it truly meets his needs or not. So why not play along? By submitting an Outback lead he's asking you to excite him about Outbacks, and to help him discover the Outback that makes him feel <u>happy</u>, not the one that meets his "needs."

- "…it's important that I speak with you…" Here's that line again! It always gives us the shivers; it's what the principal's office used to say when they called you down, and it's what the IRS and the police say when they call you in for an "interview." It sounds so stern and parental; it makes us want to run in the opposite direction. Plus, it's rather audacious is it not? Who is some car salesman to tell us it's important that we speak to him? Aren't <u>we</u> the customer? Don't <u>we</u> get to determine what is important and what is not?

- "…to determine which options and equipment are most important to you." At this very early stage in the game why are we focusing on product details? Remember your job at this point is to figure out a). Where he is in the shopping process, and b). What he's trying to accomplish with this purchase. The product part comes later. Besides, the way to find out what product items are important to a customer is to show him a product you've selected and ask "Do you like this one?" He'll quickly tell you what he likes and does not like. Grilling the customer for product specifics that he in all likelihood does not know until he sees it is likely to scare him off.

I've enclosed an e-brochure for your convenience.

Um…why? Hasn't the prospect already been on a web page somewhere that pictured and described the product? He's already seen one or more electronic brochures, why throw literature at him now? Literature he may have already seen, in fact. He is reaching out to you to help him advance himself to the next step in the sale. Why are you handing him a book and telling him to go over in the corner and read it? *From this moment on he gets all his education from you, not from sales literature!*

I will be following up this email with a phone call so that we can discuss you specific needs.

There's that "needs" word again! Only now it's beginning to make us feel "needy." At this point the prospect does not have needs - he has anxieties. "If I like the Outback will I get enough for my trade-in?" "Does the Outback fit my payment range?" "Is my credit good enough to qualify?" "Is this dealer a rip-off?" Etc. etc. etc. Our job now is not to qualify his needs, it is to ease his anxieties.

Thank you again for your inquiry and I look forward to speaking with you and for the opportunity to earn your business!

"…to earn your business!" "Seinfeld" spoofed this line 25 years ago, and it was spoof-able because consumers already found "earn your business" tired and laughable then. But, really, why is this line here? In the car biz "earn your business" really means "What price do you think I have to sell this for to make you happy?" That's a discussion to have when you are in final negations stage; this letter is an FQR! We are not even remotely at negotiations stage yet.

The salesman scored by opening with a confirmation of availability of product, and by laying out a starting price range. But what other key elements did he forget to include?
- Merchandise the product (photo and details)
- Notify the customer that you are going to advance the sales momentum and take him to the next step of the sale.

Here's an alternative General Inquiry FQR – doesn't this do a better job?

Hi James -

Good news! We have plenty of 2016 Subaru Outbacks in stock right now for you to see and drive.

Do you like this one? It is available and on sale:

2016 Subaru Outback LTD 2.5i - Stock # 1234
Exterior color: Twilight Blue Metallic / Interior color: Black.
Key options/upgrades/packages: Eyesight, power moonroof, navigation package
MSRP +$00,000
Current factory-to-consumer discount/rebate incentives -$0,000
Friendly Motors special discount -$0,000
Your Friendly Motors sale price = $00,000 + TT&L

Did you know? Subaru is offering 0.0% financing or a $000 mo. lease special on this model too. This ends soon!

You can have a free, no obligation Subaru Outback test drive today. Shall we make an appointment now? Or can I bring one by your home or workplace today instead?

I'll call you in a little bit to be sure you got this email.

Tommy Salesman

Tommy Salesman can now call and text this customer and ask for the test drive appointment without any hesitation or embarrassment because his FQR stayed on target and <u>gave value</u>.

CONCLUSION

This is where we stop today. As new materials and changing industry trends and events arrive this material will be updated again.

It has been said that the GMs and GSMs of tomorrow can be found today in dealerships' Internet departments and I have to think there is a lot of truth to that. Who would have thought a mere ten years ago that online communications and retail car sales would become so inextricably linked? But they are.

Although much growth has occurred in the last ten years this industry is far from mature. There is a lot of uncharted opportunity out there for those who see it and are willing to seize it. We hope you will be one of those people.

Thanks for reading.

Trace V. Ordiway
trace@ordiway.com
214-577-2711 v/t

http://www.linkedin.com/in/traceordiway

Made in the USA
San Bernardino, CA
11 May 2017